Snelg

95 B ⌐rescent

Red Deer, AB T4R 1K1

(Ann) 403-309-4513

Fax (403) 358-3355

MW01041718

EXIT RIGHT

*A guided tour
of succession planning for
families-in-business-together*

Mark Voeller ▸ Linda Fairburn ▸ Wayne Thompson

SUMMIT RUN, TORONTO

Summit Run Inc.
559 King Street East
Toronto, Ontario, Canada M5A 1M5
416 363 8156

© 2002 Mark Voeller, Linda Fairburn, Wayne Thompson

All rights reserved. The use of any part of this publication reproduced, trans-mitted in any form or by any means, electronic, mechanical, recording or otherwise, or stored in a retrieval system, without the prior consent of the publisher, is an infringement of the copyright law.

Published 2002. Printed and bound in Canada.

Cover desgn: Karen Petherick
Cover photo: © PhotoDisc 2001

National Library of Canada Cataloguing in Publication Data

Voeller, Mark, 1948–
    Exit right : a guided tour of succession planning for
families-in-business-together

2nd ed.
Includes bibliographical references.
ISBN 0-9687928-1-2

    1. Family-owned business enterprises—Succession.
I. Fairburn, Linda, 1952–   II. Thompson, Wayne, 1947–
III. Title.

HD62.25.P57 2002   658'.045   C2001-903170-X

Table of Contents

Acknowledgements

The authors wish to thank the following for reviewing the manuscript and providing expert feedback:

Judith Cannon, Ph.D; Jennifer Chivers-Wilson, CA; Clyde Jackson; Charles McBride, CFP; Steve Shillington, CA, CFP, TEP; George Ubels, Ph.D; Joan C. Voeller, CPA.

FOREWORD

There is a quiet crisis sweeping the world. It is not a high-profile crisis like global warming or the depletion of the ozone layer, but it is a crisis nevertheless. The crisis centers around ensuring effective succession in organizations of all types, sizes, and industry categories.

As many as 20 percent of the senior leaders in the Fortune 500 companies could retire within the next five years. The challenge lies in finding and grooming the people who can effectively replace them in a world where an aging population has reduced the candidate pool, where rapidly changing technology is redefining what it will take to manage organizations in the future, and where booming economies are making employee retention increasingly difficult.

And the crisis affects more than large, public companies. Something like 43 percent of the people who own and operate the closely-held businesses that comprise 80 percent of the North American economy are due to retire in the next five years. To make matters worse, the succession challenge can be even more complex in an owner-operated enterprise because the business must deal with the thorny question of future ownership as well as the formidable task of choosing and preparing future leadership. Add to this the family relationships that can complicate the management and ownership picture, both present and future, and it is little wonder that inadequate succession planning is a common cause of small business failure.

It is this problem of complexity that Mark Voeller, Linda Fairburn and Wayne Thompson have addressed in their little book. I call it "little" because the authors intended it to be a quick read — business owners don't have the time to wade through the hundreds, maybe thousands, of pages it would take to present a detailed, in-depth treatment of this complex subject. Besides, business owners have lawyers, accountants, insurance agents, financial planners and management consultants to fill in the details. The greater danger is getting lost in the detail and the necessarily narrow perspectives of their individual advisors. The real challenge is seeing the forest for the trees.

Hence, a "little" book; a "guided tour" rather than an exhaustive treatment; a primer rather than a textbook. And a very successful one. This little book does an outstanding job of describing the key issues in planning leadership succession and ownership transfer in a closely-held business. It is a primer that no small business owner should go without.

William J. Rothwell, Ph.D.
University Park, PA.

William J. Rothwell, Ph.D. is Professor of Human Resource Development in the Department of Adult Education, Instructional Systems and Workforce Education and Development in the College of Education on the University Park Campus of Pennsylvania State University. He has worked full-time in human resource management and employee training and development from 1979 to the present.

Dr. Rothwell is the author of *Effective Succession Planning, 2nd ed.* (2001, Amacom) and an editor of *The Practicing Organization Development Series* by Jossey-Bass/Pfeiffer.

Getting Started

You own and operate your own business. You are one of those people who enjoy the challenge of being your own boss, the master of your own destiny.

Now you are about to take on one of the greatest challenges to face any business owner — the challenge of preparing and choosing new leadership for the business and planning for the transfer of its ownership when you are gone. In short, the challenge of succession planning.

The world is full of businessmen and women who cannot escape the stress of daily operations because they neglected to prepare qualified, experienced successors.

Facing the future

Maybe you have reached an age where the word "retirement" magically has ceased being an abstract concept and become something that could actually apply to *you* — someday.

Maybe you have just had a new addition to your family and the notion of adding "& Son" or "& Daughter" to the name of the business has crossed your mind.

Maybe the notion of retirement has no appeal to you, but you're concerned about your financial security in your "retirement" years.

Maybe you're concerned about the success of family members and the continuity of your business legacy.

Maybe the death of a friend or family member — or simply driving past the remains of a horrendous traffic accident — has left you wondering what would happen to your business and your family if you were suddenly gone.

Maybe your kids are reaching an age where they are deciding what they want to do with their lives — and the possibility of a career in your business has come up.

Maybe your kids are already working with you and questions have arisen about the roles they will play in the future.

Maybe you have been developing a strategic plan for your company and realized that you couldn't plan for the future of the business without a sense of what you and your family wanted in the long term.

Maybe you have just seen your lawyer or financial advisor or insurance agent — any of them could have raised questions like "When do you want to retire?" or "Do you want to sell the business or keep it in the family?" or "How shall we treat the company in your estate plan?" or "Does your spouse want to operate the business when you're gone?" or "What would happen to the business if you died tomorrow?"

Yikes!

You can come to succession planning from any number of directions. Whatever the approach, it's a process that every business owner — particularly if the family is involved in the business — has to deal with sooner or later. And better sooner than later. The world is full of businessmen and women who cannot escape the stress of daily operations because they neglected to prepare qualified, experienced successors or failed to put the financial structures in place that would fund their retirement. Unfortunately, succession planning is a process that many business owners find difficult to contemplate. We understand. Succession planning involves facing the realities of aging and turning over control, neither of which are very high on most people's lists of favorite topics.

Beyond that, succession planning can seem overwhelmingly complex. It necessitates assessing the competencies of all involved parties. It involves personal issues, family issues and business management issues as well as legal, financial and taxation issues — all of which touch upon each other in a variety of ways. Where to start? How to proceed? Lacking clear answers to questions like these, it's easy to ignore succession planning in favor of more immediate business problems that you may feel more equipped to address.

Your willingness to confront the inevitable passing of time is in your hands. We can't help you with that except to say that it happens to everyone and effective planning can mean the difference between a smooth transition and chaos for your business and your family. Everyone grows old, but effective planning can allow you to maintain control of your destiny in your "golden" years. The choice is yours.

What we *can* do is help you get a handle on that "overwhelmingly complex" process by providing you with an overview of the major issues and some suggestions about how you can go about exploring them.

"Seeing the elephant"

The purpose of this book is *not* to provide an exhaustive treatment of succession planning, but rather to boil the process down to its essence, giving you a manageable framework for your thinking.

You've probably heard the fable of the blind men and the elephant. One man feels the elephant's leg and decides that he is touching a telephone pole. Another feels the elephant's trunk and decides that he is holding a snake. A third feels the elephant's ears and is sure that he is dealing with a banana tree. A fourth grabs the tail and is convinced that he is holding a piece of rope.

In short, each identifies the whole based on his experience of one of the elephant's parts. And of course none of them guesses that he is touching an elephant.

Succession planning means many things to many people. To some, it is an estate planning or financial planning task. To others, it is just a part of the strategic planning process. To still others, it's about ensuring that management and executive positions are filled by qualified people — a training and development task.

In our minds, succession planning is all of these things and much more. When we refer to "succession planning," we mean a process that includes strategic planning, financial planning, estate planning and the preparation of successors — all within the context of a family and within the context of a business.

In our experience, the most effective succession plans are the ones that have been developed using an integrated, holistic approach. Each part has been undertaken with the whole in mind. Our purpose in writing this book is to help you stand back as far as possible and "see the elephant" rather than delving into the detail of each of its parts.

The process

This book contains seven chapters, each devoted to one of the
key issues that you'll have to address in your succession planning:

▶ In Chapter One, *Your Second Dream*, you will explore your
vision for your future and what financially it will take to
realize your dream. Your answers to these questions could
have a major impact on all the other decisions you will
make.

▶ In Chapter Two, *All in the Family?*, you will explore your
family members' personal visions and visions for themselves
in the business. These explorations will suggest who wants to
work in the business, own the business and how family/
emotional issues might be handled.

▶ In Chapter Three, *Aligning the Business*, you will explore your
company's strategic plan and the steps the business must
take to support your personal dreams and those of your
family.

▶ In Chapter Four, *Preparing Your Successors*, you will consider
how you might go about preparing your successors for their
future roles in the family business — as executives or as
owners.

▶ In Chapter Five, *The New Leader*, you will explore the issues
related to choosing who will succeed you in the leadership
position.

▶ In Chapter Six, *The New Owners*, you will consider the business and emotional issues surrounding the transfer of the
company's ownership.

▶ And finally, in Chapter Seven, *Building Your Legacy*, you will
explore how estate planning issues can impact the entire
succession planning process.

In each chapter we identify several "key questions" you'll need to
answer. In many cases, we discuss "underlying issues" you'll need
to address as you proceed. At the end of each topic, we present
you with a series of questions to guide your "exploration" of the

issue and some suggested "action steps" you can take to move your process along.

In using the word "process," we may appear to be implying a prescribed order for your investigations. In fact, just as any of a number of situations can have brought you to succession planning, so you can enter the process at any chapter along the way. Rather than a linear series of steps, these chapters might be better seen as points on a circle, each one connected to all of the others.

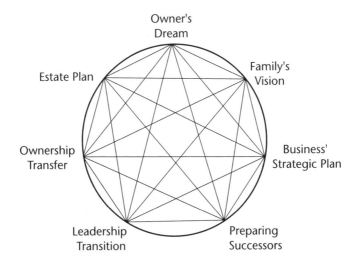

THE SUCCESSION PLANNING PROCESS

At the same time, there is a logic to the order in which we present these seven issues. We believe the true starting point should be *your* needs and those of your spouse. Only when you have a clear idea of what *you* want does it make sense to broaden the discussion out to include the desires of the rest of your family. Only when the family has developed a clear vision for its future in the business does it make sense to develop a strategic plan for the business to support the family's goals. And so on.

That being said, start wherever you're at — with an understanding that your answers to the questions in any one chapter may require some rethinking of your answers to the questions in all of the others. Understand too that your answers may change over time. While completing a plan will be an extremely valuable activity for you, your family and your business, the flexibility to allow the plan to evolve will be even more valuable.

Before we begin, a brief word on three topics that should inform all of your explorations:

▶ Systems thinking,

▶ Life cycles, and

▶ Outside advisors.

SYSTEMS THINKING

You will be doing yourself a favor if you can approach the succession planning process from a "systems" perspective.

Systems thinking is a way of viewing the world that assumes every event is complexly interdependent with other events. Changing one part of a system will change the entire system. One minor change in one system can trigger dramatic changes in any other system of which it is a smaller part, or with which it comes into contact.

The ripple effect

Much of the challenge in developing effective succession plans springs from the fact that a family business is a system comprising two major subsystems — a family system and a business system. And of course, each of these systems is made up of subsystems — right down to the individual level. A change in any one of the subsystems can have an effect on all of the other subsystems and, therefore, on the system as a whole.

Think of a pebble dropped into a pool of water. The pebble creates ripples that spread out to touch everything in the pool. Now imagine just a few pebbles dropped into two overlapping pools and you can see how powerfully and dramatically even small changes can affect the whole.

The business system, the family system and the individual family members are all in a constant state of change and development. A change in one system has ramifications for all other systems. Each system is constantly developing new coping strategies to accommodate changes in the other systems. As you embark on the succession planning process, you must keep in mind that decisions you make along the way will ripple through both the family and the business.

Fundamental differences

Family businesses are further complicated by the fact that the major subsystems — family and business — are fundamentally different.

Think for a moment about the values of a typical family. In most cases they would include such things as unconditional love for one another and the preservation of the family and its unique traditions. Put another way, the family is essentially an emotion-based system whose primary objective is to nurture and foster the well being of the clan.

In a typical business system, unconditional love is just about the last thing that you'd expect to be highly valued. Businesses, by their very nature, are goal and task-oriented and about making money. They necessarily value measurable qualities like competence, productivity and team performance.

The table below provides a brief summary of the major differences.

FAMILY SYSTEM	BUSINESS SYSTEM
Emotion-based system	Task-based system
Mission: nurture offspring into competent adults	Mission: produce profitable goods/services
Equality rules	Competency prevails
Acceptance is unconditional	Acceptance is based on performance
Relationships are permanent	Relationships are temporary and contractual
Power: generational/birth order	Power: based on authority and influence

At a very basic level, these are two different types of system, each with widely divergent written or unwritten goals and operating rules. What makes family businesses so challenging is that they must find a way for these two differing systems to co-exist under a single roof. Family business members not only must work together, they must also struggle together to keep their family's interactions harmonious.

► Sibling rivalries can be a pain in the neck for a family. But when those siblings are also involved in a family business, their rivalry can have serious business consequences — which in turn can affect the family's livelihood. From a business perspective, the rivalry must be judged rather differently than it would be if family harmony were the only thing at stake.

► The increasing eccentricity of an aging parent can be fondly accepted by the rest of the family. But when that aging parent also controls a business upon which the family relies for its economic survival, those eccentricities must be judged in a different light.

► A married person's philandering is nobody's business but his or her spouse's. But when the philanderer is part of a family business and is "fishing off the company dock" or funding his or her adventures with the company expense account, it becomes the family's business.

People have been trying for decades to build walls between these two systems — without success. These systems are joined together as a much more complex system for as long as the family chooses to stay in business together — a fact that complicates relationships and decision making for everyone involved. Devising solutions that strike an appropriate balance between business and family values is one of the great challenges of succession planning.

And if that wasn't scary enough...

Up to this point, we have been referring to the two systems that make up a family business system. Actually, there are *three* — the third system being the ownership group that can include both family members and non-family members. In either case, these individuals may or may not be actively involved in managing the business.

The diagram below depicts the interaction of these three systems to create seven different sets of circumstances for the individuals involved.

THE FAMILY BUSINESS SYSTEM
Tagiuri & Davis, 1982

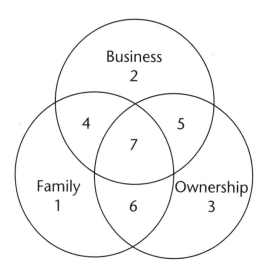

1. Family member who neither works in the business nor is a shareholder

2. Non-family member who works in the business and is not a shareholder

3. Non-family shareholder who does not work in the business

4. Family member who works in the business

5. Shareholder who works in the business

6. Family member who is a shareholder but doesn't work in the business

7. Family member who owns shares and works in the business

Individuals situated in the different segments on this diagram will have totally different experiences and expectations of the system as a whole. Different locations on this diagram will serve different needs and aspirations and are best occupied by people with different talents.

LIFE CYCLES

Another concept helpful in understanding the succession planning process is life cycles — both business and human.

Businesses typically follow a recognizable cycle that begins with *start-up*, moves on to *growth*, stabilizes at *mature* and eventually goes into either *decline* or *renewal*. The trick for long-term business success is to recognize which stage the business is in and find ways to "renew" it in the "mature" stage in order to avoid a fall into "decline."

Similarly, a family has a life cycle that follows the maturation of all its members and the "launching" of its young adults. The family life cycle can get extremely complex with multiple marriages and sets of children — often years apart in age. Finally, each member of the family is going through his or her own individual life cycle.

In a family business, all of these life cycles combine to create the unique circumstances you face in your succession planning. A sixty-two year old entrepreneur with college age children who is running a two year old start-up has a dramatically different set of interactions and circumstances than a sixty-two year old in a mature business with forty year old offspring anxious to assume the mantle of leadership.

Getting in sync

While family business leaders must follow the cycle of their own lives, they must also be aware of where the business and the rest of the family are in their life cycles. What happens all too often is that they wait too long to begin to relinquish control. The business needs the energy of the next generation. The next generation needs the wisdom and leadership of the senior generation. If you wait until old age or ill health is your operating reality, you may find that you don't have the steam to effectively play your role in the succession process, or that the handover has come too late for both the business and the next generation.

As entrepreneurs love to say, "timing may not be everything, but everything is about timing." Ideally, the senior generation is anticipating retirement while well-educated and experienced offspring are ready to re-energize a still healthy enterprise. Unfortunately, that is often not the case. Instead, in addition to the tensions of a generational shift, the business itself is forced to cope with the renewal challenge at the same time. This renewal process can be frightening to the senior generation whose retirement security is still dependent upon the successful operation of the enterprise.

Effective long-term planning can help you minimize the problems associated with personal and business life cycles that are not in sync.

Organizational change

A second challenge relating to life cycles is the organizational change that frequently must take place as the business is passed to the next generation.

Many first generation businesses are very simple in structure — the founder owns all the shares and runs the company as president or CEO. If the founder has more than one child and they all come to play a role in the ownership and operation of the business, the handoff to the next generation may require some radical organizational change to accommodate their involvement.

Moving from a single owner/leader to multiple owners and multiple leaders means a new level of complexity in the business — it's a radical paradigm shift from a monarchy to a democracy. A wrong move could mean permanent family conflict or a dysfunctional company. The choices are either to sell the business, or to give careful consideration to the roles your successors will play, and to the organizational structures required to accommodate them.

The good news is that if you are in that single owner/operator situation, the challenge is less complex than if you founded a business with a sibling, or if you and your siblings are second generation owner/operators planning to transfer the business to an even larger third generation. As the family system expands in the business, the problems of keeping everyone committed and invested in the same shared vision for the business — and happy — become increasingly more complicated.

WHO CAN YOU TURN TO?

The task of succession planning involves responsibly addressing the complexity of emotional beings who are bound together by family membership and wealth. All the while, they are running an enterprise together in a rapidly changing marketplace, dealing with issues of management and productivity, and planning for management transition and ownership transfer. Ultimately it could involve complex financial analysis, creating buy-sell agreements, conflict resolution, leadership development, creation of trusts, management assessment, and second-generation shareholder agreements — to name just a few of the very specialized tasks that routinely form part of the succession planning process.

In short, there is a ton of specialized expertise that could be required — and like most people you will probably be seeking the aid of outside consultants and advisors. Having an overview of the succession planning process will make you a more sophisticated consumer of their services.

Types of consultants

There are two types of consultant you can turn to: *expert* consultants and *process* consultants.

Expert consultants are people like lawyers, accountants, financial planners, management consultants and behavioral science consultants like industrial organizational psychologists, therapists and organization development practitioners. Each has a specialized field of knowledge. You seek their services expecting them to solve a particular type of problem for you.

The expertise that professional consultants and advisors bring from their primary disciplines is critical knowledge. But for succession planning, this alone is not sufficient. No single profession has all of the knowledge, training, education or techniques for fully addressing the total family business system. All of the tasks requiring specialized expertise in the succession planning process are interdependent parts of a larger whole.

Professional consultants with a single expertise may be limited by their disciplines. For instance, they may view the family enterprise only from a business perspective, focusing on financial and legal documents to the exclusion of the family's powerful emotional influence. Alternatively, they might view the enterprise only from a family's emotional perspective, ignoring business issues. In dealing with family businesses, experts with this kind of tunnel vision can create as many problems as they solve.

The *process consultant*, or *facilitator*, is one who assists the family in seeing the bigger picture and contributes specialized expertise to an integrated solution that moves the family *and* its business toward their own defined goals in a coordinated manner. While the expert advisor typically focuses on *what* documents to create, the process consultant focuses on *how* plans are implemented, *how* people communicate and *which* people are included.

The family business advisor

Increasingly, we are seeing a new breed of specialist called the *family business advisor.*

Typically, this is a person who begins with one of the specialized skill sets mentioned above, develops a particular interest in family business and, recognizing the complexity of the family business system, develops the knowledge and skills required to be an effective process consultant to family enterprises.

Typically, these specialists adopt a systems approach to family business problems, understand the interaction of individual, family and business life cycles, and have developed a minimum scope of knowledge from each of the disciplines that could contribute to family business solutions. At the very least, family business advisors have a strong understanding of the skill sets and tools that their colleagues from other disciplines bring to the table.

A family business advisor is not a one-stop shopping solution to your succession planning needs. Along the way, you will need to consult with a variety of experts for help that requires specialized expertise. However, if one of your expert advisors possesses the broader perspective and process skills of the family business advisor, he or she will be able to help you draw all the pieces of the process together into a harmonious whole, ensuring that you, your family and the business will be equally well served.

1

Your Second Dream

If succession planning seems complex, it's because so much of the process depends on other people. The starting point, however, is with *you*. It's your business — and your responsibility to ensure that it can survive your sudden death, disability or retirement. More importantly, it's your life — and as a business owner, it's your privilege to decide how your business can help you create the life you imagine for yourself.

The world is full of retired business owners who have discovered they're bored silly by the life of golf and gin rummy they had planned for.

You had a dream of running your own business. Now, we'll ask you to consider a second dream — a dream for life *after* the business.

Of course, the succession planning process is not just about you. In the course of this process, you will have to deal with assumptions and expectations held by your offspring or other family members. We'll get to these considerations in future chapters, but for now, put them aside and focus on *your* heart's desire. Too often, family business owners put so much effort into meeting their obligations to their families that they never get around to considering their own needs.

That's why we suggest that before you do anything else, you explore your own long-term desires for both your life and your business. If you are married — or some other modern equivalent — you would be well advised to undertake your visioning process in collaboration with your spouse or significant other. You may have to revisit your dream in the light of family and business realities. But at least start with a dream. If you don't have one, you could find that you are the only one whose needs aren't met at the end of the day!

Key Questions:

Exploring your "second dream" amounts to answering three — and possibly four — key questions:

▶ How do you want to spend your "golden" years?

▶ What will it take financially to live your dream?

▶ Do you want to keep the business in the family?

...and if the answer to this question is "yes"...

▶ Can you make the shift from "me" to "we"?

In the following pages, we will explore each of these questions in more detail.

Underlying Issues:

Your answers to these questions involve a world of possibilities — but however you go about it, the process will require:

▶ self-awareness,

▶ a willingness to plan, and

▶ the ability to let go.

We'll consider the impact of these underlying issues as we explore the "key questions."

KEY QUESTION:

How do you want to spend your "golden" years?

Very simply, if you don't know where you want to go, you aren't likely to get there. Sometimes it's fun to just wing it — many terrific vacations have started with nothing more than gassing up the car and choosing a point on the compass. But we're talking about what could amount to *a third of your life* here — it would be foolhardy to leave financing it to chance. And in order to put together a sound plan for retirement, you need to know what you will be financing.

In short, a realistic and compelling vision of life beyond business for you and your spouse is the foundation for your succession planning process. Without that vision, the answers to all of the questions that follow will be mere guesswork.

Do you want to retire completely? Do you want to retain some involvement in the business? Do you want to become involved in other businesses? Do you want to move to someplace smaller? Warmer? More exotic? Do you want to sail the seven seas? Do you want to golf every day? Do you want to become involved in charitable or philanthropic activities? The possibilities are endless.

Here's where self-awareness is crucial. The world is full of retired business owners who have discovered they're bored silly by the life of golf and gin rummy they had planned for. The world is also full of business owners who are so reluctant to face a life without work — or other structure — that they never get around to retiring. Understanding yourself well enough to know what you really want to do next is absolutely critical to the succession planning process — and of course the same holds true for your spouse.

This is also where your ability to let go is so important. Ten percent of owners say they'll never retire — and this is one of the options for you to consider. To retire, you'll need the ability to find meaning in your life after giving up the challenge, influence, status, identity, control and daily structure of running your own business. Can you honestly say you can live without all of that?

This is one of those places in the process where a behaviorally oriented business consultant such as a psychologist could be of service. Understanding what you want seems simple enough, but in fact, the simplest questions are often the hardest to answer. A skilled professional can help you explore your own desires and motivations.

Explorations:

▶ Do you have a vision for your life 10, 20 and 30 years from now?

▶ Does your spouse have a vision for her or his life 10, 20 and 30 years from now — with or without you?

▶ Do you wish to step away from business entirely? Do you see some limited role within the business as providing structure for your life?

▶ Does your spouse wish to step away from business entirely?

▶ Do you have interests or hobbies that can structure your time and provide you with meaning and satisfaction if you're not involved in the business?

▶ Does your spouse have interests or hobbies that can provide structure, meaning and satisfaction if she or he is not involved in the business?

Action Steps:

▶ Undertake an assessment of your human, financial and time resources.

▶ Develop a post-retirement picture for you and your spouse.

▶ Determine what role, if any, you and your spouse will play in the business.

▶ Find out whether your spouse harbors a desire to maintain control of the business after you are gone.

KEY QUESTION:

What will it take financially to live your dream?

Once you have developed a vision for your future, you can begin planning to ensure that you and your spouse have the financial security to live your dream.

The first step is to determine just how much money it will take to finance your vision — this will provide you with a meaningful starting point for any discussions about ways of extracting your equity from the business.

Obviously, this is a point in the process where input from your accountant, insurance advisor and/or financial planner will be helpful. It is also one of those points in the process where your willingness to plan becomes important. Planning can be a difficult and often tedious process, but it is necessary. It takes time to create the circumstances that will allow you to pursue "life after business" — and for the business to continue on successfully without you. This won't happen without careful planning. Determining what it will take to pursue your envisioned lifestyle brings focus to all of your planning.

Many business owners resist planning because it can be anxiety-arousing. Planning is about addressing the ambiguity of the future with all its uncertainties. Succession planning is about addressing the inevitability of change. Ambiguity, uncertainty and change are all major stressors, so it's understandable that most of us would rather not think about them. But the fact is, stepping up to these issues and making some decisions about them can *reduce* stress.

It may be that you can't fully answer some of the questions. Don't let that stop you.

All plans evolve over time — but they can't evolve if you don't begin the process. Make a start *and write it down*. Putting your thoughts on paper makes them more concrete and increases the chances both of your continuing the process and taking action based on your conclusions. Behavioral research reports that effective change is highly correlated with written documentation. As long as you remember that they are not written in stone, written plans can help you move forward.

Explorations:

▶ Are you willing to write out answers to these explorations?

▶ How much money will you and your spouse need to pursue your preferred lifestyle?

Action Steps:

▶ Create a computer document or loose-leaf notebook and commit to recording your responses to the exploration questions and your plans of action as you work through this book.

▶ Develop a realistic budget for the kind of life you envisage for yourself and your spouse.

KEY QUESTION:

Do you want to keep the business in the family?

A number of factors will influence this decision.

Financial considerations

On a purely financial level, you will have to determine whether it is feasible to transfer ownership of the business to your family and still finance the life you wish to lead in retirement. There are any number of ways of unlocking your equity in the business asset, but you may find that the only way to provide the resources you need is an outright sale to someone with cash in hand. Obviously this has implications for any dream of keeping the business in the family.

Family considerations

Furthermore, to carry on the business successfully, your family members have to *want* to do it. Your passion for the business has undoubtedly been a key contributor to its success — do you sense that the next generation either possesses or lacks that same "fire in the belly?"

You also will need to consider whether the family members who will take over the business have the ability — or at least the potential — to operate it successfully. Too many family businesses flounder in the second generation because the founders had a bad case of "kennel blindness" — the inability to realistically judge their kids' abilities. This is particularly important if you will be financially dependent in your retirement on their ability to operate the business.

We'll be exploring the implications of the above issues in the following chapters. For now, the question is "what is *your* heart's desire?" For some owners, the business is simply a means of making a living or creating wealth. For others, it becomes something more — their passion, their creation, and their legacy. They want to see it carried on under the family name and are willing to make great effort and sacrifice to see this happen. How do you see your business? What do you want for it in the years ahead?

Explorations:

▶ If you had to decide now, would you sell the business or try to keep it in the family?

▶ Are you being realistic in imagining your family carrying on the business?

▶ Do you have a vision for the business 30, 50 and 100 years from now?

▶ Is it important to you that the business remains in the family? Why?

▶ What role would your spouse wish to assume in the business if you suddenly died or became incapacitated?

Action Steps:

▶ Clarify your own vision for the business beyond your stewardship.

▶ Clarify your spouse's expectations regarding the business.

▶ Evaluate the potential of your family to carry on the business without you.

▶ Share your visions with each other.

KEY QUESTION:

Can you make the shift from "me" to "we"?

If you envision your family carrying on the business, you have many steps to take to ensure a successful handover. The first of these steps is an internal one — making the shift from "entrepreneur" to "family business owner." We frequently refer to this as a shift from monarchy to democracy.

If you are like most people who founded a business, you began with a dream of personal independence and control over your life — not with the dream of creating a collaborative team of family members seeking to build an ongoing, multi-generational venture. In short, you were the classic independent entrepreneur — and for the classic entrepreneur, succession is truly the ultimate challenge.

Rather than seeing your business only as your passion and personal playground, you must also view it as an entity with a life cycle separate from your own life course. You and your spouse need to adopt a collaborative approach with a commitment to continuity and a tolerance for change and differences.

Making the shift

The successful entrepreneur is a self-directed, action-oriented decision-maker. To be a successful family business leader requires a somewhat different approach. It requires open communication with all family members, a collaborative approach with all family in management and a loosening of controls so the potential successors have an opportunity to practice leading. Developing an understanding of organizational behavior through additional education or reading, or by working with a behavioral science consultant, can go a long way toward helping you make this transformation a reality.

Success follows when you can embrace a vision of the business as a legacy that will live on and change with the passage of time. As a consequence of embracing that vision, you will have to create opportunities for the next generation of leaders to learn, to assume real responsibilities and to make decisions — and errors.

You will have to identify successors who are committed to the vision of the family business as a legacy. You will have to encourage their defining a strategic vision for that business.

We will be exploring these issues in subsequent chapters, but for now, the key issue is your willingness — and ability — to let go of the total control you have enjoyed.

Explorations:

▶ Do you require total control of the business to feel comfortable?

▶ Can you change? Do you want to?

Action Step:

▶ Seek a professional assessment of your management style, paying special attention to the degree to which you allow others — particularly family members currently involved in the business — the autonomy to make decisions.

2

All in the Family?

The succession planning process started with you and your spouse clarifying your own needs and desires regarding your futures and the future of your business. The next step is to broaden the planning process to include your family members.

Unresolved conflicts and emotional issues are the most frequent reasons cited for family businesses failing to negotiate the transition from one generation to the next.

Even if your family is not involved in the business, this is a necessary step. If you died tomorrow, your family would inherit the business as an asset of your estate — without a plan to cover these circumstances, the business could be thrown into chaos. For the sake of the business, a plan should be in place to allow it to function successfully under your heirs' ownership.

If family members are involved in the business, or if you foresee them becoming involved, their participation in the planning process is even more important.

Key Questions:

At this stage in the planning process, there are two key questions you need answered thoughtfully and honestly:

▶ Do members of your family have a vision for their own lives?

▶ Does the next generation wish to own and/or operate the business?

Underlying Issues:

Underlying both of these questions are three aspects of succession planning so crucial to effective transitions, and to family business success in general, that we will deal with them before we tackle the key questions.

▶ The value of a family council,

▶ The importance of open dialogue, and

▶ The importance of healthy family relationships.

UNDERLYING ISSUE:

The value of a family council

Throughout this book, we will refer to the family council as a vehicle for facilitating open dialogue and healthy relationships. The following provides some detail about what a family council is and why we highly recommend developing one for your family.

What is it?

A family council is a formal, periodic meeting where family members share information, discuss issues and make decisions about matters that affect them as a group. You can have a family without having a council, but if you are a family-in-business-together, a family council is a valuable tool for enhancing family relationships and improving communication.

If you think back to the "three circles" model of the family business system discussed in the introductory section, the family council can be seen as the forum for the family circle. While a management meeting will involve family members with a management role in the business, and a shareholders' meeting will involve family members with an ownership role in the business — not necessarily the same people — the family council includes all family members regardless of their role in the business. It can also involve those who may not have a direct involvement in the business but who are nonetheless affected by its direction and success.

In short, the family council is the organizational and planning arm of a family with direct links into the business. It is the place where the whole family meets to:

▶ share information about the business;

▶ set policies, make decisions, and establish directions for the future that affect the whole family and their business; and to

▶ surface and address interpersonal concerns of an emotional nature that influence the family — and, therefore, affect the business.

At its best, a family council becomes a forum for ongoing dialogue among family members that supports healthy, open and inclusive communication behaviors. This ideal is rarely achieved without help. Families-in-business-together successfully using a family council almost without exception strongly recommend using a facilitator skilled in dealing with family dynamics and conflict.

Why develop one?

In a family enterprise, family members are the single most important influence upon the business' planning. The personal goals of family members, therefore, critically affect the direction of the company. A family council can help both family and business by:

- ▶ identifying the goals of those involved;

- ▶ formalizing the family's commitment to the company's future; and by

- ▶ shaping the vision of that future for both the business and the family.

Unresolved conflicts and emotional issues are the most frequent reasons cited for family businesses failing to negotiate the transition from one generation to the next. It follows that interpersonal issues are the single most important influences affecting a family-owned business. The family council serves to help minimize interpersonal conflicts that might interfere with business decisions by:

- ▶ providing a forum for sharing and learning about one another's personal circumstances — this permits greater sensitivity and consideration in decision making;

- ▶ clarifying business decisions that have been misunderstood;

- ▶ clarifying personal decisions that might have been misunderstood by others;

- ▶ including family members who are not active in the business or those who have felt like outsiders; and by

▶ providing a forum to mediate the personal and other conflicts that arise in all families.

What does it look like?

A family council is not a single meeting but rather a monthly or
quarterly forum for considering the complex issues facing a
family in business. It's a sequence of chaired meetings that for-
malizes the informal exchanges that take place among family
members.

The format of a family council meeting can be either businesslike
or casual. The agendas are generally set by a family member —
the family council *convenor* — in consultation with the family's
facilitator or family business consultant. Families generally select
a convenor who is comfortable dealing with interpersonal issues
and has working relationships with all branches of the family.
Frequently, the convenor role is the first leadership role for a
potential successor. The convenor role can be rotated according
to a family agreement.

Generally speaking, family councils:

▶ meet regularly — usually 4-12 times per year;

▶ are formal gatherings — often with minutes, guidelines,
procedures and a charter;

▶ have membership that is open and inclusive, usually involving blood relatives and possibly in-laws — and having possibly a minimum age requirement;

▶ function as an advisory group to clarify, communicate, and
inform its members;

▶ represent the family interests on the business' board of
directors; and finally

▶ provide guest speakers on any topics of interest to family
members i.e. family history, interpersonal skills training,
management training.

What are its products?

Commonly, family councils produce four kinds of documents: a statement of family values; a family mission/vision statement; a code of conduct; and a family charter.

Values Statements — explicit statements of the principles and values that the family holds important and intends to adhere to as its members approach life, solve problems and make decisions.

Family Mission/Vision Statements — short philosophical statements that describe the family's commitments to its members and its community as well as outlining a vision for the family's legacy and future.

Code of Conduct — a set of guidelines for interacting with each other whether at home, at work or in the community. It frequently is used by a facilitator to resolve existing conflicts, and is good preventive medicine for potential disharmony.

Family Charter — a family governance document that sets out explicit guidelines so as to minimize the likelihood of conflict related to suspicions of favoritism, unrealistic expectations or lack of "fairness." It may include the values and mission statements described above as well as:

▶ *Entry Policy* — rules for entering, participating, and remaining in the business;

▶ *Compensation Guidelines* — an understanding of how family members will be compensated and a general statement regarding the distribution of dividends; and

▶ *Succession Guidelines* — usually the founder's statement regarding his or her current beliefs about succession planning and his or her biases regarding stock ownership.

Explorations:

▶ Does your family have a vehicle for exploring controversial or emotional issues affecting the family or the business?

▶ Does your family have a written code of conduct for communication and interaction?

Action Steps:

▶ Find a "process consultant" who can facilitate family communication events.

▶ Organize a family council to discuss emotional family and/or business issues and develop a vision for the family.

▶ Use the facilitator in family council meetings to address any issues identified in the following explorations.

▶ Assess your family members' shared understanding of policies and plans in order to identify unspoken assumptions, expectations and inadequate information transfer.

▶ Develop a code of conduct for communication and interaction.

▶ Use the family council or a facilitated retreat to develop consensus on issues that will affect the business like the family's values, the family's vision of the business, community responsibility, how it will govern itself, general plans for ownership and how business leadership will be selected.

UNDERLYING ISSUE:

The importance of open dialogue

Effective communication is perhaps the most crucial issue in succession planning. It allows differences to be settled, problems to be solved and relationships to flourish. Most importantly, it allows the planning process to proceed on the basis of facts rather than assumptions.

▶ How can your family know what you have in mind for the business if you don't share your vision with them?

▶ How can you know what role, if any, your family members wish to play in the business if you don't ask them — and if they don't share their visions with you?

▶ How can you prevent family relationships interfering with the business — and business relationships interfering with the family — if you don't communicate openly and honestly with each other?

Assess your skills

There isn't a person alive who couldn't improve his or her personal communication skills. And most families have developed some poor communication habits — or lack of habits — which can haunt the business and the succession planning process.

Very early on in the process, therefore, you will do well to assess the communication skills and practices of your family — as individuals and as a group — and take appropriate steps to improve communications.

Develop vehicles for communication

Family councils, facilitated family retreats, written codes of conduct and communication skills training are all vehicles for improving communications. These activities may seem like a lot of effort, but in our experience, most families benefit from hashing out ground rules that promote open dialogue and from taking formal timeouts for communication.

As mentioned previously, research shows that these processes are significantly more effective when facilitated by a skilled outsider. Find a facilitator who has an interactive style compatible with your style and with your family's. Make sure the facilitator has sufficient experience with family systems and with the business considerations covered in the balance of this book.

Explorations:

▶ What is your family's process for exploring challenges facing the business or the family?

▶ Does anyone in your family have difficulty communicating effectively about personal issues affecting the business? Entertaining differing viewpoints? Does anyone provide a positive model?

▶ Do differences in communication styles hamper interaction among family members?

Action Steps:

▶ Have an outside consultant explore your family members' communication styles and develop strategies to minimize miscommunication and perceived offense.

▶ Assess your family members' willingness to communicate with each other about personal or business issues.

▶ Have family members, yourself and your spouse included, take a communication skills training course.

UNDERLYING ISSUE:

The importance of healthy family relationships

A study of the factors associated with successful transitions in family businesses published in a 1997 issue of *The Journal of Business Venturing* indicated that *60 percent* of succession break-downs are attributable to problems in relationships among family members.

Small wonder!

A business ultimately is a group of people tied together in a complex series of relationships — as is a family. Mix business relationships and family relationships and the complexity seems to increase by leaps and bounds. Family relationships affect the business; business relationships affect the family — both for good and ill.

The family is made up of individuals who have relationships based on years of emotional connection and shared experience. Relationship problems are created by experiences and assumptions made during the years of growing up together. Those same assumptions then color the individual's perceptions later in life and in totally different contexts — for example, in business.

Misunderstandings and inaccurate assumptions about the motivation of others frequently lead to hurt feelings, resentments and festering rivalries. Without some vehicle for resolving differences, those hurts, resentments and rivalries will inevitably interfere with critical business decisions.

In the end, the key to a functional family business and a successful transition from generation to generation is a functional family.

Explorations:

▶ Are there current family issues impacting the business that need to be resolved? Sibling rivalries? Alcohol or substance abuse? Emotional or mental problems? Attitudes of entitlement? Abuses of power? Abundance of, or lack of, skills or abilities.

▶ Are there existing business conflicts among family members? Conflicts regarding compensation, ownership or desire to buy parts of the business? Overt or covert signs of an inability to report to each other, to share ownership or to work as a team?

▶ Will the succession planning process create challenges for the business or for the family? Have those challenges been discussed openly?

▶ Does your family have a process for resolving disruptive differences or misunderstandings?

Action Steps:

▶ Assess the relationships among your family members and how they might impact the business.

▶ Take the necessary steps to promote healthy family relationships.

KEY QUESTION:

Do members of your family have a vision for their own lives?

One of the great things about owning a business is that it can provide a means of securing your children's future. Not only does it let you to put food on the table when they are growing up, but it allows you to provide them with ready-made careers.

Unfortunately, this gift can be a double-edged sword. Too frequently, the offspring of business owners enter the business to please their parents, or because they don't feel they have a choice. The result is a second generation that either runs the business with half a heart or dies a slow emotional death because they have never had a chance to follow their *own* dreams.

Too frequently, members of the second generation are cast in roles for which they are ill suited or again, for which they have no passion. There seems to be an unwritten rule that offspring must become presidents or general managers when in fact, they might be more effective and happier in other roles, such as research, marketing or human resources.

Too frequently, the family business provides a line of least resistance — a safe haven from the potential of failure your children would have to face if they had to make their own way. The result can be a generation that lacks the confidence and sense of accomplishment that comes from taking on the world successfully.

Too frequently the children of business owners harbor feelings of entitlement. Such attitudes can wreak havoc with employee relations. They also can lead to serious family rifts if your ultimate decision about who will lead the business does not jibe with your offspring's assumptions about their future roles.

In short, assumptions — both on your part and on the part of your family members — can have a negative impact on the business and on the lives of everyone in the family. The antidote is open, honest and deliberate communication about the individuals' desires for their lives and the business.

Ideally, a family will wholeheartedly support the desire of any one of its members to pursue a career path outside the family business. When offspring feel supported in their options to seek personal fulfillment, there is usually less "entitlement" and greater support for the family's succession plan.

Explorations:

▶ What does your family know about your visions for your future and the future of the business?

▶ What do your family members want to do with their lives? Do their visions include involvement in the business? What are their preferred roles?

▶ Should family members continue to be involved with the business?

▶ Are any of you making assumptions about each other's visions of the future that you haven't actually confirmed?

Action Steps:

▶ Share your vision with the rest of the family.

▶ Have each of your family members develop a personal vision and ask them to share their visions with the family as a whole.

KEY QUESTION:

Does the next generation wish to own and/or operate the business?

The issue of who is committed to keeping the business in the family is probably one of the most important questions facing the individual family members. A related and even more sensitive topic has to do with who is committed to family ownership if he or she is *not* running the business.

The last exploration will have told you whether your family members want to make careers in your business, but it doesn't necessarily help you decide whether to sell the business or plan for the family to maintain ownership.

Owning shares in a business and operating a business are two different things. Some or all of your family members may not be interested in operating the business, but they may be comfortable with the prospect of reaping a share of the profits of an ongoing concern. Or, they may prefer their inheritance in a lump sum up front, or in the form of non-business assets.

When it comes to estate planning, understanding the wishes of your heirs will allow you, if you choose, to make a plan that best serves both them and the business.

Ideally, the family has fostered autonomy and self-assuredness in each of its individual members. That autonomy should allow each family member to clearly state his or her level of commitment to keeping the business in the family.

Explorations:

▶ What are your family members' wishes regarding working in and/or ownership of the business?

▶ What assumptions do your family members hold about job entitlement? About compensation levels? About obligation to work in the business? About eventual ownership?

▶ Can family wealth support education for alternative career choices?

Action Steps:

▶ Determine the wishes of each potential successor regarding working in and/or ownership of the business.

▶ Ask what assumptions your family members hold about job entitlement, compensation levels, obligation to work in the business and eventual ownership.

3

Aligning the Business

In the previous two chapters, the focus was on people — specifically, you and your family members. The goal was to identify what each of you envisioned for your life and for your future involvement in the business. And, you may have synthesized a statement in your family council that represents your family's belief about its shared purpose and its stewardship of the business asset.

In this chapter, the focus shifts to the business itself.

*The issue here is not **how to create a strategic plan, but whether your business' plan is aligned with your family's vision.***

Clearly, the futures you and your family members have envisioned for yourselves will be possible only if the business remains successful. In these times of rapid change, past success does not necessarily ensure future success. Therefore, this chapter focuses on the process that businesses employ to clarify their strengths and weakness, develop strategies for long-term viability and identify the expertise or systems they need to achieve their goals — strategic planning.

Not only must the business remain successful, but it also must be moving in a direction that supports the needs you identified in the first two chapters. Strategic planning is your opportunity to align the directions the business is taking with your desires for your own future and that of your successors. It's a chance to integrate a complex set of family considerations with business strategies.

Presenting a detailed treatment of the strategic planning process is far beyond the scope of this book. The issue here is not *how* to create a strategic plan, but whether your business' plan is aligned with your family's vision, and whether it has taken your family's ownership and participation needs into account.

Underlying Issues:

That being said, we will briefly discuss the *value* of strategic planning for the simple reason that most businesses haven't done it — or having created a plan, haven't implemented it.

▶ The value of strategic planning

We will also encourage you to consider creating a board of advisors — non-family executives, entrepreneurs or professionals who can provide valuable input about changes in the marketplace and developments in other industries. They can broaden your network of resources and perhaps most importantly, can provide objective input and valuable perspective around business decisions that can become emotion-laden because of family dynamics.

▶ The value of a board of advisors

Key Questions:

The strategic planning process challenges you to answer a number of questions about the business' purpose, strengths, weaknesses, business environment, goals and directions. Within the context of succession planning, there are three key questions to ask:

▶ Does the company's strategic plan support the family's vision and values?

▶ Is the business positioned for long-term viability and succession?

▶ Could the business survive your untimely death or disability?

UNDERLYING ISSUE:

The value of strategic planning

What is it?

Simply put, strategic planning is the process of developing a plan of action that defines how an organization will use its resources to gain a competitive advantage in its larger environment. Typically, this includes choices about the functions an organization will perform, the products or services it will provide, and the markets and populations it will serve.

In the business setting, the process involves a series of management meetings that include key employees and active family members who systematically study the business and the market it serves. The study is sometimes referred to as a "SWOT" analysis in that it seeks to identify the company's *strengths* and *weaknesses* and the *opportunities* and *threats* in the marketplace. The results of the study provide a foundation for setting meaningful long-term goals and determining the best strategies for attaining them.

Usually strategic plans contain the following five components:

▶ *Mission* — who you are; the purpose of your business.

▶ *Vision* — where you want to go.

▶ *Values* — how you will act as you pursue that vision.

▶ *Strategy* — how you will get to where you want to go.

▶ *Tactics* — specific action points for implementing strategy.

The benefits

Strategic plans are valuable to a business because they provide an overall framework for short-term planning and day-to-day decision making. They provide a "map" that ensures that everyone in the business is moving in the same direction — and moving in the direction which offers the best chance for success.

For family businesses, there are some additional benefits. To begin with, developing a strategic plan will set you apart from most of your competitors. According to research findings by Arthur Andersen/MassMutual in the United States and Deloitte & Touche in Canada, 75 percent of the family-owned firms in those countries have no strategic plan or other written planning document. Unfortunately, smaller family-owned businesses frequently neglect the discipline of a formal planning process that considers changes in the marketplace, technology and product lifecycle — issues that will determine the ongoing success of the business operation.

Strategic planning discussions can revitalize the operations of a family business that has become mature and possibly stagnant over the years. Having a strategic plan and sharing it with key stakeholders — including family members — creates trust and confidence in the leadership of the company.

In short, developing a strategic plan for your business can be a major step toward ensuring that it will be able to meet your retirement needs and the needs of the next generation — *if* those needs have been taken into account in the strategic planning process.

Don't forget the people issues

Too often, strategic plans focus on product development and marketing but ignore the human capabilities required to make the rest of the plan work. This is a major oversight in any strategic plan, but it can be even more damaging when succession planning is part of the picture. One of the most important questions in strategic planning is "Who has the competence to implement the strategic plan?"

Your SWOT analysis should include a thorough examination of the capabilities and potential of current employees, including family members involved in the business. The analysis should pay particular attention to the members of your leadership team, present and future. Your strategies should cover what the company will do to ensure that your human resources will be adequately developed for the eventual transition to a new generation of owners and managers.

Explorations:

▶ What is happening in your industry? New products? New competitors? New technologies? Changing consumer demands?

▶ What economic and/or political and regulatory changes have implications for your enterprise and for your successors?

▶ Where are your products or services within their lifecycles?

▶ What are your company's strengths and weaknesses? How can you build on the strengths? What can you do to address the weaknesses?

▶ Does your company have the human resource capabilities it needs to go forward?

Action Steps:

▶ Conduct a thorough review of trends in the marketplace, including the activities of your competitors. Look for opportunities and challenges.

▶ Conduct a thorough review of the strengths and weaknesses of your business.

▶ Conduct a thorough review of your human resource capabilities.

UNDERLYING ISSUE:

The value of a board of advisors

In a traditional business structure, the organization is owned by shareholders, guided by directors and operated day-to-day by officers. In many family businesses there is a tendency to wear these hats simultaneously without distinguishing amongst these three roles.

- ▶ The *shareholders* are the financial risk takers who expect to profit from their investment in the company.

- ▶ The *directors* make decisions and establish policies on behalf of the shareholders to which they report. Declaring dividends, building a new plant, and expanding territory or product lines are all examples of the scope of the directors' decision-making authority.

- ▶ The *officers* — president, vice president, secretary and treasurer — report to the directors. These are the people who run the company. While they have full authority for day-to-day operations and implementation of the strategic plan, some of their decisions require the participation of, and approval from, the directors.

The intention behind this formal governance structure is the conscious separation of ownership from management because these two groups have potentially conflicting interests. Shareholders are generally more interested in short-term profits and dividends. Management, on the other hand, might be willing to sacrifice short-term profits to achieve long-term goals.

The problem is that in family businesses, members of these two groups also share membership in another group — the family. The conflicting interests of the ownership and management groups can have serious implications for family unity. It's easy to imagine non-active family shareholders coming to loggerheads with managing family shareholders over the question of what to do with the year's profit.

The second problem is that in many family businesses a relatively small group of people occupies all of these positions. The result can be "tunnel vision," one of the most common afflictions among family business people. As any business owner knows, simply keeping up with the work at hand can be more than a full-time job — it's easy to lose track of what's going on beyond your company and your industry. One entrepreneur calls it "the habit of working *in* the business interfering with working *on* the business."

A board of advisors can help you address both of these problems.

What is it?

The purpose of a board of advisors is to provide advice. Its strength lies in the fact that many of its members come from outside the confines of the family — this allows them to provide you with objective input in emotionally loaded situations as well as an infusion of experience and perspective from the "outside world." It is a step up from the "kitchen cabinet" that served you so well in the start-up years and a step down from the responsibility and legal liability of a formal board of directors. The power of an advisory board is limited to whatever authority you chose to bestow. It has no legal obligations. Its members do not necessarily hold stock. It can neither hire nor fire the officers. Its purpose is to ensure the health of the business by:

▶ participating in the succession process;

▶ reducing conflict and inappropriate favoritism;

▶ reviewing compensation policies for family employees;

▶ approving transactions that appear to benefit some family members more than others, such as the purchase or sale of an asset;

▶ reviewing financial policies such as declaring dividends; and last, but not least

▶ telling the truth on difficult issues.

Especially in a small company, having a board of advisors is a considerable asset. When creating your board, it is wise to follow the ratio of one external board member to every family board member. In addition to setting policies, a board that includes outside experts can help to bridge conflicts and speak the truth about difficult subjects such as succession planning, successor selection and other needed changes.

What does it look like?

Your business is best served when the board of advisors includes members of each of the following groups:

▶ *Company executives* — who hold stock, executive management positions, or both

▶ *Non-active family members* — who are liaisons, serving as representatives to your family council, and

▶ *Non-family members* — who have business experience and who are compatible with your family members.

Whether you're constituting your first board or replacing retiring board members, here are some criteria for membership consideration.

Experience — Potential members should have experience in business or on boards. While some businesses include their professional advisors — for example their accountant or lawyer — we generally suggest that professional advisors serve in their independent capacities in order to avoid any conflict of interest. Thinking of the future, you may want to include business leaders who are a step or two ahead of you in business. Non-family managers or officers make good additions to your board too.

Compatibility — The ideal board member presents no conflict of interest, complements your talent and skills, and is someone who you would trust with your business and financial information. They should be compatible with your personality, values and philosophy.

Time — Your external advisors need to have enough time to be prepared and to be present, both physically and mentally, at meetings. From time to time you may want to consult with your advisors about unexpected important matters that come up in business.

Interest — In addition to having the time, your board members should also have an interest in your industry, dedication to the interests of your business, and sensitivity to your family issues.

Conflict-handling skills — Advisors who are level headed and objective while still maintaining sensitivity to your family issues can be enormously helpful. Select individuals who are comfortable confronting and openly exploring family issues affecting the business.

Your board should meet in person at least two times per year but four is better. Prior to the meeting, all board members should receive the proposed agenda as well as the pertinent financial and business records. Board members often receive compensation for their time and reimbursement for travel expenses to attend meetings.

Exploration:

▶ Would your business benefit from a board of advisors? Who would be appropriate? Do you have any fears about exposing your business and your leadership to "outsiders"?

Action Step:

▶ Consider creating a board of advisors.

KEY QUESTION:

Does the company's strategic plan support the family's vision and values?

In the last chapter, we suggested that you form a family council to generate some written statements regarding what the family holds to be important and the role the business will play in the family's future. These statements should become a major input for the business' strategic plan. After all, a family business exists to serve the family's interests. It is, therefore, important that the business' strategic plan take into consideration the family's needs and align its vision, values and mission with those of the family.

In a publicly-owned business, the critical question is how best to address the marketplace to generate acceptable shareholder value. In a family-owned business, the critical question is how best to address the marketplace in a way that is consistent with family values, and that ensures the financial security of the owner and participation of the successors. In short, a family-owned business must address a somewhat more complex set of issues in its strategic planning.

The mission statement

An effective *mission* or *purpose* statement should clearly define why the business exists. Such a definition is only meaningful if it tells you what the business is meant to do for those who hold a stake in it — shareholders, employees and customers. Clearly, the family is a major stakeholder. The mission statement must, therefore, include the benefit the business brings to the family as well as to customers and to the community. If the benefit defined in the business' strategic plan is at odds with the benefit defined by the family, you're setting yourself up for trouble down the road.

The vision statement

A *vision* statement defines the long-term goals of the business. Again, if the business' goals do not reflect the goals articulated by the family, it will be difficult for the business to serve the family members' long-term needs. The family's vision for the business has clear implications for options such as growth, participation in a consolidation or roll-up within an industry, or for specialization versus diversification. It also has implications for the type of leadership the business will need as the transition to the next generation occurs.

It is not uncommon for a family-in-business-together to assert that the business exists in order to create financial prosperity, but never at the expense of family harmony. Other families hold that part of the purpose of the business is to keep the family together. The implications of either position for long-term planning can be enormous — therefore, the positions must be explicitly stated.

The values statement

Finally, if the business' *values* are not aligned with the family's values, at the very least you risk a situation in which the family is uncomfortable with the way the business operates. In the worst case, you create philosophical differences that could tear the business apart somewhere down the road. Family values such as "contribution to the community" or "preservation of the environment" can have a real impact on business decisions and must be taken into account.

Explorations:

▶ What does the family expect from the business? Is this expectation reflected implicitly or otherwise in the business' mission statement?

▶ What are the family's long-term goals for the business? Are they reflected in the business' vision statement?

▶ What values do the family hold dear? Are they reflected in the business' values statement?

Action Steps:

▶ Develop a mission, vision and values statement for the business, using your family's mission, vision and values as a starting point.

▶ If your business already has mission, vision and values statements, review them for consistency with your family's statements and revise them if necessary.

KEY QUESTION:

Is the business positioned for long-term viability and succession?

The final components of a strategic plan are strategy and tactics. Mission, vision and values define who you are, where you want to go and how you will act along the way. Strategies and tactics define how you will get where you want to go.

The ideal strategy for your business will match your family's goals, will build on competitive strengths, is relatively easy to implement, doesn't pose a high risk of creating problems with employees, customers or suppliers, and is affordable.

You need to determine what resources you'll require to implement your strategies. Remember that resources in the broadest context include human resources and time, not just money. In the new economy, resources can also include your ability to access knowledge, new employees and strategic partners.

To ensure the success of your planning efforts you must also plan for their implementation. You need to determine a budget — a step in the planning process that is often omitted. You'll want to make sure there are sufficient funds available for you to make choices, develop your successors and fund your retirement.

Your willingness to share information, include others in the process, and plan for the future of your business has already put you in the top quarter of all family businesses. You may want to give yourself another leg up on the competition by submitting your plans to your board of advisors who can raise pertinent questions and offer differing perspectives.

Explorations:

▶ Has your business developed strategies for achieving its long-term goals?

▶ Have your strategies taken succession issues into account?

▶ What changes have to be made to make your strategies work? To products and services? To product delivery? To customer service? To human resources? To marketing? To the organization?

▶ What financial resources are required for achieving the vision and strategic plan you have outlined? How will you acquire those resources?

Action Steps:

▶ Develop a set of strategies to support your long-term business and succession goals. Review existing strategies to ensure that they will meet the family's needs.

▶ Create a budget for implementing your strategies.

KEY QUESTION:

Could the business survive your untimely death or disability?

The first two questions in this chapter can be answered in the process of strategic planning. The third question requires a different kind of planning — crisis planning.

The difference between strategic planning and crises planning is the length of time between the event and the reaction. Your sudden death or disability would create a crisis, a situation that requires immediate and effective action.

The difference between day-to-day problems and a crisis is that a crisis is not anticipated. There is an element of surprise. By its very nature, your untimely death or disability will contain the element of surprise. But your business does not have to be surprised by the issues that will be raised in these circumstances. You may not want to think about the answer to this question, but your business will be better off if you do. You can't control fate, but you can prepare the business for its consequences.

Issues that typically arise include:

▶ Who will run the company?

▶ The need for a board of advisors.

▶ The need for a named and trained successor.

▶ The impact of the owner's personal guarantee on banking/supplier relationships.

▶ The reliance of the business on the owner's personal relationships with bankers/suppliers/clients.

▶ Who is the executor of the owner's estate? Implications of the executor's fiduciary responsibilities on the business.

Explorations:

▶ Who will take control of the operation of your business in the event of your untimely death or disability? Are they prepared? If not, what can be done?

▶ What changes in organizational structure would have to be made if you suddenly weren't there?

▶ Does the business rely on your personal financial guarantees? How would the business' operating finances be affected?

▶ How would your untimely death or disability affect employee/vendor/customer relationships? What steps could be taken to reassure them? What can be done now?

▶ Will your insurance arrangements see the business through or does your business have sufficient debt capacity?

Action Steps:

▶ Conduct a simulation to identify how your untimely death or disability would affect the operation of the business.

▶ Review or prepare a contingency plan for operating the business in the event of your untimely death or disability.

▶ Review banking relationships, credit with suppliers, guarantees on long-term notes, etc., to ensure viability in the absence of your personal guarantees or assets.

▶ Consult with your insurance advisor regarding your options.

▶ Make sure that someone has been designated as acting CEO and has signing authority.

4

Preparing Your Successors

You and your spouse have identified long-term goals for your lives and for the business. You have communicated your wishes to the family and determined what visions they hold for their lives and for their involvement in the company. The business has developed a strategic plan to ensure that it is on track to support the family's vision. In this chapter, we will address the process of preparing the next generation to play their future roles effectively.

Your blood in their veins does not guarantee that your offspring will have what it takes to successfully assume your mantle.

Start early!

The key point to make here is that you should be preparing your potential successor(s) long before you make the actual succession decision. The good news is that you may have already begun this process years before you started reading this book — by instilling in your children attitudes about hard work, dedication to values, sensitivity to others and integrity. Throughout the life of your business you have been developing your employees.

The next stage of succession preparation began when your offspring first worked in your business as part-time or summer employees. That was their first experience with training, accountability and handling relationships with other workers.

Up to this point, the process has been fairly informal. Somewhere between summer job and full-time employment, however, you and your family need to do some thinking — and some talking.

Key Questions:

Having laid a foundation for the family in the second chapter and having created a strategic plan for the business that will prepare it to meet the family's needs in the third chapter, you now have three questions to answer regarding the preparation of your successors:

▶ Which family members will enter the business?

▶ Who will you prepare for succession?

▶ How will you prepare them?

Underlying Issue:

However you answer these questions, there is an issue that members of your family will face as they join the business. We call it

▶ "the offspring's burden."

UNDERLYING ISSUE:

The offspring's burden

Offspring of families-in-business-together frequently have access to sophisticated business experiences far earlier than their peers. They are often given significant business responsibility and authority at a much younger age. In this regard, they are lucky. However, with these blessings come burdens.

▶ For starters, there is the burden of responsibility that they will have to shoulder sooner than their peers. Attempting to explain the burden that goes with the blessing to peers is impossible — they simply see the offspring as fortunate to have such opportunity.

▶ Then there is the opinion of those who see them as the beneficiaries of nepotism and not deserving the responsibilities they receive.

▶ And finally, they are evaluated by parents and by non-family executives who often continue to see them as if they were youngsters in knickers. Frequently, they are given very little credit for competencies demonstrated — those who view them as "the youngsters" simply point out all there is yet to learn.

For many offspring, working in the family business can seem to be a losing proposition. What is the potential successor to do? And what can you do to help them deal successfully with the unique position that they are, literally, heirs to?

Lightening the load

You can draw up performance expectations that will help ensure that they meet the same standards and receive the same support as their non-family counterparts. This will at least remove any legitimate grievances on the part of their peers and the frustration that comes from being held to a higher standard than anyone else is. But this will not change the fact that the happy accident of being your offspring has given them unusual opportunities. Nor will it change the fact that some non-family members will be envious. Either can lead to a sense of unworthiness that can undermine your offspring's effectiveness and happiness.

Coping successfully with the offspring's burden requires a strong sense of self — the knowledge of what they want, what they know and what they can do. It requires sufficient self-esteem to retain their sense of confidence in the face of mistakes in judgement. It requires assertiveness — the ability to state their position and ask for what they need. How to help them develop these qualities is the subject of whole libraries — well beyond the scope of this book. We can, however, make several suggestions.

▶ Being aware of the difficulty of their position can help you avoid contributing to the problem.

▶ You can help them gain self-awareness through mentoring, feedback processes and the use of personal/professional coaches.

▶ A behaviorally oriented consultant could be of real value by helping your offspring understand and cope with the "dark side" of their blessing. It's not easy being "the owner's kid." A professional who understands their situation and is equipped to help them successfully carry their special burden could make an enormous difference to their peace of mind and to the long-term health of the business.

▶ Most important of all, you can encourage your family members to assume personal responsibility for their own development and to take charge of their futures. There is nothing but pain if they wait for the "benevolent dictator" parent to take care of them because they have been loyal to his direction and to his expectations. Make sure that your offspring are joining the business because they truly want to, not because they wish to please you or because they have an ensured job.

▶ Require them to go out into the world and acquire their own experiences and successes before joining the business. Defining their own worth in situations where they don't have the advantage of being the "owner's kid" will give them the resilience they'll need to cope with the offspring's burden once they join the business.

▶ Allow them the freedom to change their minds.

▶ Encourage their choice of management development or Executive MBA programs, and YPO or Sons of Bosses (SOB) experiences.

KEY QUESTION:

Which family members will enter the business?

You began to answer this question in Chapter Two when you asked family members to share their visions of their futures with you. Taking that step can help you avoid what experience suggests to be one of the most common mistakes in succession planning — an inaccurate assessment of the next generation's motivation. Open dialogue among family members can help you proceed based on accurate assumptions.

The issue of desire

Ask yourself and your family whether everyone who wants to be involved with the business has been included. Ideally, everyone with the desire and the necessary competencies should be extended the same invitation and opportunity to work in the business and to eventually rise to a position of leadership. And the invitation must be made overtly. It may seem like restating the obvious, but what is clear to you may not be clear to others. Younger children, for instance, may assume there isn't room for them in the business unless they are clearly invited.

Likewise, it is important to show your support and respect for those who prefer to pursue their own dreams outside the family business. Active involvement in the business should be seen as an option, not as an obligation. The family should be clear about the premise that each individual will be supported in their pursuit of their own interests, whatever they may be.

The issue of ability

So far, we have been dealing with the issue of *desire* — are family members interested in pursuing a career in the business? To be effective, however, they require more than desire — they require *ability*.

Family loyalties are a wonderful thing, but it's hard to run a successful business if family ties are the only qualification for employment. Similarly, your blood in their veins does not guarantee that your offspring will have what it takes to successfully assume your mantle. It should be clear that leadership positions must be earned, not inherited — and that successors should not feel obligated to assume leadership positions if executive roles are not where their talents or interests lie.

Create an entry policy

Many families address this issue by setting criteria that family members must meet before they are eligible to join the business. Establishing a policy, through the family council, for entering the business can encourage both entries into the business and a sense of fairness to other family members and employees.

Some of the factors you might consider for your policy include:

► minimum age level,

► minimum education level,

► work experience outside the family business,

► written job description with real responsibilities,

► fair wages for the work and compared with other employees, and

► supervision, if possible, by a non-family member.

There is an additional benefit to setting an entry policy. Too often, family members enter the business right out of high school or college because it is the line of least resistance. Both they and the business can suffer from their lack of further education or work experience in the outside world. By requiring them to meet educational and work experience requirements, you ensure that they bring more to the business when they finally enter it, and you give them a chance to grow and develop outside the protective environment of the family. Moreover, their accomplishments elsewhere boost their credibility within the company and can be somewhat effective in deflecting charges of nepotism.

Explorations:

► What are the potential successors' visions for their lives and their roles in the business?

▶ What criteria should family members meet before they are allowed to enter the family business?

▶ How can the business ensure that family members perform adequately?

▶ Does the next generation understand the roles and responsibilities of ownership — even if they will not be involved in management?

Action Steps:

▶ Review potential successors' expectations and needs for both responsibility and financial security.

▶ Use your family council to develop a policy for family members entering the business.

▶ Create explicit job descriptions and a process for holding every family employee accountable.

▶ Develop clear policies for compensation and termination.

KEY QUESTION:

Who will you prepare for succession?

There are two schools of thought on this issue for your family and business to consider. One school holds that you can never prepare too many family members for leadership — because you can't predict what twists and turns life holds for your family and its business. The other school holds that clarity is the primary concern — early designation of the successor-elect reduces hostility that can arise out of unmet expectations. Each school of thought has valid arguments — it will be up to you to decide which approach best fits your circumstances.

Develop succession criteria

Choosing your successor can be a task so complex, so awesome that many business owners choose to avoid it all together. There are many factors to consider. You can avoid complications by developing generic criteria for succession as many years in advance as possible — updating them as circumstances or the marketplace changes. The criteria amount to a list of minimum qualifications for the job.

Having generic succession criteria reduces the potential for conflict, especially where there are several candidates for a single position. They establish a sense of fairness and increase stakeholder confidence in your management of the business. And, defining clear criteria for succession increases the likelihood that the potential successors will begin developing the skills, knowledge and ability for the job early in their careers.

Some qualifications for succession might include:

▶ the expectation that the candidates possess a minimum amount of education or experience within your industry,

▶ have relevant prior work experience outside the company, and

▶ have worked inside your business in positions of increasing responsibility.

Use your family council

You can use your family council to work out the emotional issues that might come up during this process. You and your family will want to express and clarify one another's wishes about the role each wants to play in the business and their expectation regarding position, responsibilities, income and lifestyles. And at the very least, your crtiteria will give direction to the process of preparing possible candidates.

Don't forget to share the criteria with family and key employees. This allows each offspring — as well as non-family employees — to more easily accept the ultimate decision as being fair and logical rather than a demonstration of favoritism. It also allows your offspring to assume personal responsibility for pursuing their own development plans.

Don't forget non-family members

Up to this point, we have been talking about preparing successors only in terms of family members. In fact, you should consider what your succession might look like in circumstances where you can't decide on a family successor or where family candidates are too young, not available or unqualified.

Succession planning is not a process exclusively for family-owned businesses. In publicly-owned businesses, it is a process for developing and promoting the most talented people to ensure that vacancies are smoothly filled and that leadership positions are filled by the people most qualified to hold them. This is also true of family-owned businesses, and you will need to stay open to the roles that non-family members can play, and to the possibility that the best interests of the business — and ultimately the family — may be served by a non-family member taking over the helm from you.

And don't forget the ownership role

Furthermore, succession planning is not just about preparing the future leader. It is about preparing *everyone* for the roles they will ultimately play in the business. For family members this could include the role of non-active shareholder.

Whether heirs plan to work in the business or not, they need to learn about the realities and responsibilities of business ownership. Wise business families create a system for teaching offspring basic concepts of business ownership and management like the following:

▶ the role of management;

▶ the kinds of capital needed for the successful operation of a business;

▶ how net profits differ from gross revenue;

▶ how dividends may fluctuate from year to year;

▶ the need to provide shareholders with a return on investment;

▶ the need to provide non-active shareholders with some access to their capital; and

▶ the long-term benefits of re-investment.

In short, you would be wise to ensure that your potential successors thoroughly understand their options as potential owners and that those who envision an active role in the business thoroughly understand and embrace their fiduciary responsibility to non-active shareholders.

Explorations:

▶ Will the business develop a pool of possible leaders or designate a single individual?

▶ What criteria must the next leader meet?

▶ Do potential non-active owners understand the consequences of being a minority shareholder without a voice in active management?

▶ Do the potential active owners understand their fiduciary responsibilities to their non-active shareholders?

Action Steps:

▶ Create succession criteria.

▶ Solicit input from the board of advisors and, if appropriate, the family council.

KEY QUESTION:

How will you prepare them?

Having made your decision about your "succession pool," the next step is to create a plan for developing those individuals so that they will be prepared to take over when the time comes.

In our experience, entrepreneurs have difficulty with this process. You are successful because you have the "right stuff" — the combination of knowledge, abilities and attitudes that lead to success. Typically, you do what you do instinctively and tend to forget that getting it wrong was part of learning how to do it right. You grew with the business and so did your job description.

However, if you want a seamless transition, you are going to have to anticipate the competencies your successors will need and take steps to help develop them. Moreover, you will need to accept the fact that you yourself may not possess the qualifications required by your successors, who will be facing an entirely different set of challenges.

This is where a career planning consultant can come in handy. A competent professional can help you define "the right stuff" for the key positions in your organization — identify the "competencies" required for success — and help you with the process of making sure your successors acquire those competencies.

The process

There are three basic steps to this process.

First, you need to identify the skills and experience your successors will need — the succession criteria we suggested you develop a couple of pages ago.

Next — as suggested back in Chapter Two — assess your offspring to determine their current competency levels and to identify what skills and aptitudes they possess so these can be nurtured. Remember skills or aptitudes that seem useless now might represent a huge competitive advantage to the firm tomorrow. Regardless of their age, encourage your children to speak openly with you about their career or succession interests.

The third step is to determine how best to help individuals bridge the gap between their current levels of competency and those they will need to successfully carry on the business. Again, a career planning consultant can be of value here. Some of the options they might suggest would include:

- ▶ defining possible career paths for your successors — a progression of related jobs, each with more responsibility, that facilitates the development of seasoned leaders;

- ▶ creating job descriptions and performance expectations and setting up a process for regular reviews — a significant step you can take to enhance the preparation process, and for that matter, overall performance in the business if it is done for all employees;

- ▶ identifying further educational and training opportunities that will augment the on-the-job training;

- ▶ receiving exposure to others in similar situations through trade association groups and family business forums;

- ▶ developing enhanced industry knowledge through seminars and trade group meetings; and

- ▶ gaining leadership experience by assuming responsibility for special projects.

Again, don't forget that offspring who are not going to be working in the business may someday have an ownership role. To play that role effectively, they will need to understand their responsibilities.

Explorations:

- ▶ What aptitudes and skills do your offspring, and other employees, possess?

- ▶ What management skills will the business need to meet the challenges identified in your business' strategic plan?

▶ Who will need what preparation in order to assume the responsibilities?

▶ How will you ensure that each individual acquires the skills and experience they need?

▶ Who will hold family members new to management roles accountable for their performance? How will that process be accomplished objectively?

Action Steps:

▶ Create a human resources plan with a mandatory evaluation period.

▶ Create an educational process so that each potential successor understands the options, entitlements and responsibilities of ownership.

▶ Identify competencies and/or experience required to implement the business' strategic plan.

▶ Assess the skills, abilities and motivation of each potential successor.

▶ Define a personal/professional development plan for every interested family member and for key employees.

▶ Consult your board of advisors for their input.

5

The
New Leader

Around the time you reach age sixty, your family, your employees and people with whom you do business start wondering what your plans are. During this stage of your life, and in this phase of your business' lifecycle, there is a great deal of anxiety in the system.

If you are like most business owners, you'd rather have a root canal than surrender your decision-making authority.

Your executives and the next tier of management have many questions about your plans for succession and their personal opportunities for advancement. Your customers and distributors are concerned about your business' stability and ability to perform in the years ahead. Your vendors are concerned about their relationship with you and their share of your market. Your bankers are wondering who will be financially responsible if something happens to you and how credit-worthy the next management team will be. And all of them are probably wondering if your heirs are prepared to be competent owners and exactly who will be leading and managing the business in the future.

In the previous chapter, we explored the steps you can take to ensure that the next generation of owners and leaders of your family business are prepared to assume their roles. Now we turn to one aspect of the final phase of this process — selecting a leader to succeed you and smoothly transferring control of the company's operation.

Do it sooner rather than later

Generally speaking, it is better to choose your successor sooner rather than later because effective family business leadership transitions don't happen overnight — typically, they take five years, or more.

Why so long?

- ▶ Because it takes more time than you think to develop the requisite skills to run a business as complex as yours is, or will be, by the time you're ready for retirement.

- ▶ Because when you publicly announce the change of command there will be repercussions — some of which you will have anticipated and some that will just take time to sort out.

- ▶ Because choosing your successor can trigger a phase of organizational renewal activities with accompanying intergenerational projects that help prepare everyone for new leadership.

► And finally — and this may be the most difficult to orchestrate — because you want the development of your successor to coincide with the readiness of the business for new leadership and with your readiness to step down.

Are you ready?

That last phrase — "your readiness to step down" — deserves an additional comment. If you are like most business owners, you'd rather have a root canal than surrender your decision-making authority. Many find it easier to give up ownership than to giving up management control — even a little. This can be an enormous impediment to a smooth leadership transition because if you don't marry authority to increasing responsibility, you risk demoralizing your successor and confusing everyone else in the company. Worse still, you could compromise your successor's training, because until the new leader has actually exercised the power, his or her experience won't be complete.

In Chapter One, we encouraged you to ask yourself whether you were ready to make the change from "me" to "we." Now you have to take that a step farther and ask yourself whether you are ready and willing to actually let go.

Key Questions:

Your willingness to surrender control may be the key issue for the entire succession planning process. It certainly becomes crucial at the leadership transition stage, and could require some real soul-searching. And meanwhile, you have two key questions to answer:

► Who will run the business?

► How will you ease the transition?

KEY QUESTION:

Who will run the business?

In the good old days, anything worth inheriting went by custom or by law to the eldest son. The practice is called "primogeniture" and, while it made the succession question a slam dunk, it was also responsible for the lost fortunes of half of Europe's titled families and more than a few monarchs who could have used another dip in the gene pool.

Surprisingly, some family businesses still operate on the assumption that the eldest son automatically comes equipped with the wherewithal for business leadership. Perhaps they haven't learned from history. Perhaps they are using an age-old custom to avoid a difficult choice. While the first reason is just plain dumb, the second is understandable — choosing a successor might be one of the most difficult decisions a family business owner has to make.

For any business leader, selecting a successor is a serious task — the future of the business depends upon it. For you, it's doubly difficult because you are also a parent required to judge the worthiness of your child or children, often having to select one over the other.

Your options

The good news is that you do not have to stand alone in this decision. You can use the outside members from your board of advisors to help you manage the selection process and make the actual decision. In fact, if you go to these board members for no other reason than this, they will have done you a great service. Involving your board in the selection process ensures an unbiased evaluation of the successor's competence. And, perhaps most importantly, it helps to create consensus about who will assume the leadership of the organization.

Whether you go it alone or make it a board decision, you have five basic choices:

▶ pick one or more of your children or other family members;

▶ select a key non-family manager;

▶ create a top management team and hope a leader will emerge;

▶ recruit someone from the outside; or

▶ appoint interim management for a limited tenure to develop young offspring and select a permanent successor.

Choosing one of these options, and then choosing the appropriate individual, will be a lot easier if you go about the process deliberately.

Develop leadership criteria

The first step is to identify competencies the new leader will require above and beyond the general succession criteria you have already developed.

Start by determining what kind of leadership the business needs for the years ahead. Will you need an entrepreneurial leader to go after new markets and develop new product or service lines? Will you need a managerial leader who can ensure stability and efficient operation? The strategic plan you developed in Chapter Three should help you make this decision.

Then decide what specific qualities and skills the type of leader you envision will need. This will allow you to set criteria against which to assess the capabilities of the various possible candidates. By setting clear criteria for the new leader's position, you make it possible to make an objective selection.

Develop selection guidelines

These include a description of the process that will be used for selection. That process can take many forms:

▶ You can make the decision entirely by yourself;

▶ You may want to place the decision in the hands of your board of advisors;

▶ You may want to bring in qualified outsiders to assess the candidates and abide by their decision; or

▶ You may use a combination of all of these approaches.

One way or another, the key is to use the criteria you have developed as a benchmark against which to measure the candidates.

One way or another, it is important that you communicate the process that will be used to all concerned. This will help the non-successful candidates accept the ultimate decision as having been fairly made.

And don't forget the runners-up!

Additionally, you will want to give some consideration to how you will retain the interest and loyalty of those who haven't been chosen. Family members not chosen for the leadership position can easily become resentful or simply lose interest. Incenting key non-family employees who must live with the fact that they may never be eligible for the ultimate prize is one of the perennial challenges of the family business. Creating career paths with ample opportunity for professional growth and financial reward for those you don't choose for the leadership position will go a long way towards ensuring that these key people both stick around and give their best efforts.

Explorations:

▶ What process will be used to select the next leader?

▶ What type of leader will the business need in the years ahead?

▶ What qualities and skills will the ideal leader possess?

▶ Is there a family member who meets these criteria?

▶ What roles will family members not chosen for leadership play?

▶ How will the family handle new roles for some family members?

▶ Have successors earned the respect of non-family executives and employees?

▶ Do key executives have a clear picture of opportunities for advancement that are still available for them?

Action Steps:

▶ Develop selection guidelines — in concert with your board — defining who will select the next leader, using what criteria and when.

▶ Openly discuss the criteria that will be used for successor selection.

▶ Openly discuss this proposed plan with all family members as many years in advance as possible.

▶ Do active career planning with all non-family managers.

▶ Create incentives to ensure their continued motivation.

KEY QUESTION:

How will you ease the transition?

Choosing the new leader can be such a difficult experience that you will be tempted to breathe a sigh of relief and hurry back to the daily routine once the decision has been made. In fact, choosing the new leader is only the beginning of the transition process. It is important to give as much consideration to planning and implementing the transition of your chosen leader as you did to the selection process. If not, the new leader will begin his or her tenure at a disadvantage.

Complete the CEO-to-be's training

The first thing your plan should cover is the final stage of your successor's training. If you have followed our advice up to this point, you have long since created development plans for your key employees and your offspring. New leaders drawn from this group should have a sound foundation for their new responsibilities. Now you want to put the final touches on their preparation by easing them into the position and letting them take their solo flights while you're around as backup.

Create an on-the-job development plan for the CEO-to-be based on formal assessments that include recommendations for addressing weaknesses, setting goals, and a schedule for review by the board. The CEO-to-be should continue his or her professional studies, learning practical business skills, and developing a professional network outside of the business. Your successor needs to hone the ability to think strategically — and the best way to learn this is to run a division of the company with bottom-line responsibilities that involve hiring, firing and making a profit. And one last thing you should expect from the next generation is that they get and stay current with personal computers and industry-relevant technology.

Plan organizational changes

Way back in the introductory section to this book, we talked about the possible need for organizational change to accommodate the next generation and the opportunity for organizational renewal often associated with succession. This could involve any or all of:

▶ developing new business strategies;

▶ realigning the formal business management systems; and/or

▶ building a new management team.

You addressed these issues in your strategic planning process in Chapter Three — now the job is to plan and implement the changes envisioned for the leadership transition. Placing this initiative in the hands of your successor not only takes advantage of the energy of the younger generation, but also associates the changes with the new leader. This allows them to put their mark on the company in the eyes of everyone associated with the business. Beginning the change process while you are still around will help minimize the anxieties of employees, suppliers and customers by signaling that the change has your blessing.

This is another one of those points where the services of an organization development professional can be valuable. An OD consultant can help you envision the changes that are required, present the steps you wish to take to both family members and non-family employees, and track the implementation of the transition plan.

Create a timetable

Another key component of the transition plan is creating a time frame — and sticking to it! Making and following a time-bounded process for succession creates credibility and confidence in you, builds trust in your family, and energizes the succession process.

Communicate the plan

And finally, once you've chosen the new leader, tell people. Tell everybody about it!

For starters, tell your family. There might be some disappoint-ment, even surprise, but it is better to make your choice known and handle the dissenters now rather than later. Making the selection process transparent rather then secretive will help you avoid surprises and create stakeholder buy-in as you go along.

Tell your customers, suppliers and creditors. By this time, hopefully these parties will not be strangers to your successor. Some of them may even have been consulted and will welcome him or her into the chair. Again, if this is not the case, it is better to know as soon as possible so their concerns can be addressed.

Finally, tell your employees. All of us create our future in the present by the choices and commitments we make. Every day, your employees are reflecting their commitment to your company based on their impression of the future. In times of change, people get very insecure and your employees are no exception. If they don't have the facts they'll probably make them up. And worse yet, frightened employees can react by joining your competition, becoming your competition or forming unions.

How you communicate is just as important as *what* you communicate and *to whom* you communicate. Differences in style or approach need to be recognized and respected — as do varying needs for input, acknowledgement, structure and control, and differences in reaction to stress. Miscommunications during this transition period can create unnecessary apprehension and tension. The use of a behavioral or organization development consultant who is skilled in assessing interactive styles, needs and reactivity can dramatically ease your transition.

Step aside

One final point about the transition plan: make sure that everyone is clear about *your* future role, responsibilities and authority — including you. Step aside only when you are ready to stay aside.

We have seen many supposedly retired family business owners become bored with their new lives after a couple of years and start hanging around the business, often giving orders and otherwise "helping out." Unless the terms of your involvement are clearly defined, you can create confusion among the employees and undermine the authority of the new leader. Spell out your new role and stick to it. You'll spare yourself, the new leader and your employees some difficult situations.

As you approach this major transition in your life, it's crucial for you to remember the implications it will have for a lot of other people's lives — and that those people may be experiencing a good deal of anxiety about what the future may hold. Giving them a clear idea of where you and the business are heading is both good business and a personal kindness.

Explorations:

▶ What further action can you take to ensure that the new leader is fully prepared?

▶ What steps can be taken to initiate organizational renewal? What role will the new leader play in implementing them?

▶ What changes will be required in management structures?

▶ How will you communicate your choice of the new leader to family members, employees, suppliers and customers?

▶ When will the transition be complete?

▶ What will your role be when the transition is complete?

▶ Can you work without disruptive conflict with the chosen successor when he or she attempts to assume more responsibility and authority?

Action Steps:

▶ Obtain an assessment of workplace styles and needs for all current and future members of the management team.

▶ Actively negotiate evolving roles for yourself and the selected leader(s), identifying evolving sets of responsibilities at each stage in the transition process.

▶ Create a plan for the transition period.

▶ Set a timetable for implementing the plan.

▶ Communicate the plan to all stakeholders.

▶ Publicly announce your own retirement date.

▶ Attend to the needs of other family members' careers.

6

The
New Owners

Being in business is like being in a canoe. Why? Because there are two times when you can really get into trouble: getting in and getting out. In the last chapter, we considered one aspect of "getting out" of the leadership role. Now we consider a second aspect of "getting out" — the transfer of your ownership of the business.

Many business owners try to treat their family members fairly by giving each an equal share in the business. This well-meaning practice can create a world of pain.

There's a fair chance that you jumped directly to this chapter — the questions of who will own the business in the future and how the transfer of ownership will be accomplished are often what brings a business owner to the succession planning process in the first place. If family business owners are going to go looking for outside input on any issues relating to succession, it will probably be this one — ownership transfer.

If, in fact, this chapter is your point of entry, we urge you to backtrack and work your way through the earlier steps. Your answers to the key questions in previous chapters provide you with much of the input you require as you address your options for ownership transfer.

In Chapter One, you explored your vision for your future and what financially it would take to realize your dream. Your answers to these questions will affect when and how you transfer ownership.

In Chapter Two, you explored your family members' personal visions and their visions for themselves in the business. The results of these explorations will suggest who wants to own the business in the future and how family/emotional issues regarding ownership might be handled.

In Chapter Three, you explored your company's vision and the steps the business must take to position itself to support your personal dreams and those of your family.

In Chapter Four, you considered the steps you would need to take to prepare your successors for their future roles — including ownership — in the business.

And in Chapter Five, you explored the issues related to choosing who would succeed you in the leadership position. You will need to come up with an ownership formula that does not undermine future management.

In short, the first five chapters lay a foundation for considering ownership issues. If you have not completed these explorations, we urge you to do so. If you have, we suggest that you revisit your conclusions from previous chapters in the light of the ownership questions that you are about to consider.

Key Questions:

The ownership aspect of "getting out" boils down to two key questions:

▶ When will the change in ownership take place?

▶ Who will own the business?

KEY QUESTION:

When will the change in ownership take place?

You have three basic choices here:

▶ ownership can change incrementally, starting while you are still active in the business;

▶ it can be transferred at the point of your retirement, or

▶ it can be transferred on your death.

As you will see in the next chapter, you will have to make provision for the latter one way or another to protect your family and the business in case of your untimely death. But for now, let's assume that you are going to live to a ripe old age — in which case the first consideration is how you are going to fund your golden years.

When people who spend their working years as employees retire, they have savings and pension plans that hopefully allow them to live comfortably. As a family business owner, your financial picture may be somewhat more complicated. You may have personal assets sufficient to fund your retirement — in which case you are in the happy position of having the choice of how best to transfer the business.

But, if you are like many family business owners, most of your personal wealth is tied up in the business. To reduce your personal taxes, you may have found ways for the business to take care of many of your needs and more than a few of your pleasures. Rather than taking the profits out of your business, you may have left retained earnings in the company to fund future growth or capital expenditures.

And now you look to the company to meet your needs and pay for your pleasures in retirement. Again, you have three basic choices, each with advantages and disadvantages in terms of financial security, tax burden and personal cash flow:

▶ sell out gradually,

▶ sell out in one fell swoop, or

▶ retain ownership, collect salary/management fees, consultation fees and the usual perks, and then let your stock transfer to your heirs on your death.

You will want to examine these options carefully with your family advisors to determine which ones best meet your personal security and cash flow requirements.

You will also do well to examine these options from the point of view of the future health of the business. Maintaining ownership and requiring it to meet your ongoing financial needs could place the company in a difficult financial position, particularly if a replacement for your position is required.

Explorations:

▶ What do you need financially to pursue your vision for your life after work?

▶ What options do you have for achieving the personal financial position you need?

▶ Which of those options works best for you, the family and the business?

▶ How much control do you wish to retain until you have achieved your financial objectives?

Action Steps:

▶ Consult your financial advisors to accurately determine your future financial needs.

▶ Consult your financial advisors regarding possible options for realizing the money you need from the business.

▶ Consult your management consultant/family business advisor regarding implications of the above options for the business and the family.

KEY QUESTION:
Who will own the business?

Succession planning as a process involves the transfer of two kinds of control: management control and ownership control. In a family business, these two ultimately have to be considered together if you are to create an ownership/management formula that best serves your personal interests, the family's interests and the interests of the business.

Some of the obvious combinations of ownership and management control available to you and your family include:

- ▶ retaining management and ownership within the family;
- ▶ hiring outside management and retaining ownership within the family;
- ▶ sharing ownership with outside management;
- ▶ selling the business and hoping the new owners retain your offspring in management;
- ▶ selling the business and reinvesting in another business;
- ▶ selling some or part of the business to employees, and
- ▶ going public.

The business perspective

As you consider these options from a business perspective, the key issue to keep in mind is the importance of marrying ownership with management. Many business owners try to treat their family members fairly by giving each an equal share in the business. This well-meaning practice can create a world of pain. Here's why.

A time-honored prescription for effective business management holds that CEOs should maintain responsibility and authority over their business decisions and be able to profit from them. Many advisors encourage business owners to distinguish between potential active and non-active heirs and to limit ownership to those who will actually be in control of the profit picture.

Typically, non-active shareholders, just like those in a public company, are most interested in their dividends. Active share-holders, on the other hand, are more likely to take a long-term view and are willing to re-invest profits. Unless the non-active owners are personally invested in the growth and long-term survival of the business, this difference in perspective can lead to conflict and anger — to the detriment of either the business, the family, or both.

Placing ownership and management in the same hands will avoid potential conflict. This can be achieved through a plan allowing offspring who will manage the business to purchase the company. The proceeds from the sale can then be bequeathed to your heirs. Or, it can be achieved through an estate plan in which active family members receive shares and non-active family members receive non-business assets.

Unfortunately, you will not have the latter option when the bulk of your assets are held within the business and have to stay there for the health of the company. You may be forced to give all of your children participation in the ownership of the business. In this case, you have to decide whether controlling interest should be given to those active in the management of the business and whether those who are taking the risks and making the decisions should profit to a greater extent than those who are non-active in the business. Estate freezing, business reorganization and issuing different types of shares can help achieve this strategy.

The family perspective

Up to this point, we have been considering the ownership deci-sion from a business point of view. As with all decisions in a family business situation, you will have to consider the owner-ship transfer from a family perspective as well.

First, there is the question of what your family members actually want. If there are significant assets outside the business, it would seem logical to pass ownership of those assets to those family members not involved in the business, and to give ownership of the business to those working in it. However, the wishes of family members, surprisingly, are often different. Consider these scenarios:

▶ Those active in management sometimes see the potential downside of the business and prefer to inherit assets outside the business that they perceive as more liquid or stable.

▶ Those not working in the business may want to own a minority position for a variety of reasons that are purely emotional. To them, the business may be symbolic of their connection to you. It may reflect their need to feel connected to their siblings through their participation in the family business. It may have subjective meanings related to status in the community or family, to their identity, or to their sense of self worth. While these are not logical business considerations, they nonetheless could affect your children's ability to enjoy each other as family or to successfully cooperate as mutual owners of your business.

▶ Family members can become sensitive if they feel they are being left out. Their logic is: "because we are all family, we all should be treated equally with the same unconditional love without regard for business realities, performance realities, or the realities of effort and contribution."

▶ Other family members may fear that the existing family business has a greater potential than other assets they might inherit, so they want to participate in that asset. This is a powerful emotional consideration that does not take into account the very real downside of any business venture or the severe limitations of liquidity that the minority ownership could entail.

▶ Some less than effective or unsuccessful family members assume that ownership entitles them to a job — and a well-paying job at that. This value system can burden the business, rob that brother or sister of the opportunity to be successful in his or her own right, and position the next generation for serious emotional conflict and unhappiness.

Interpersonal considerations

In addition to your family members' wishes regarding ownership, you will also have to consider their personality and interactive styles and the implications this might have for them working together as co-owners of the business. The reality is that some siblings will always have difficulty making decisions together without disruptive conflict and confrontation. This type of strife leads to distancing, if not outright alienation. Sharing ownership for this group does nothing but threaten family harmony and the business' performance.

Other siblings rather enjoy the challenge of debate and conflict, and use that process to explore various creative alternatives. After seemingly heated exchanges, they apply the emergent knowledge to find general consensus and then go to dinner together. Differences and conflicts for these individuals are positive.

Alternatives to co-ownership

After exploring the emotional issues of shared ownership as described above, you may want to consider some of the following alternatives if they are available to you:

▶ splitting the business,

▶ buying another business, or

▶ providing ownership or leadership roles in another family enterprise.

Preparation is everything

These considerations return us full circle to Chapter Four where we discussed the preparation of all family members for the eventual process of succession and asset transfer. Non-active owners must have enough knowledge to understand the realities of running a business while those who are active in managing the business must have a strong sense of their fiduciary responsibilities to minority shareholders. Both must share a commitment to the family's philosophy regarding entitlement versus responsibility. And ideally all parties will have developed strong communication skills and a willingness to participate in structures like the family council.

These considerations also return us to the importance of communicating with your family members as discussed in Chapter Two. *You* need to know what they really want. *They* need to understand your thinking on the eventual ownership of the business.

When you start talking ownership, questions about equality and fair treatment will assuredly surface. These emotional factors are the unique challenges faced when transferring ownership and doing estate planning within a family-owned business.

If you haven't established a family council, go back to Chapter Two and reconsider the incredible value of this type of governance structure for a family-in-business-together. Use your family council as a forum for surfacing and addressing unmet expectations and emotional reactions and for explaining your own biases about what is best for the business and therefore for them.

And make use of the non-family members on your board of advisors, both for an objective assessment from a business perspective of what is in the best interest of all your heirs, and to help communicate the ownership plan. Frequently, family members find it easier to put aside their emotional reactions and consider the business reason for a decision when an objective outsider presents it.

Explorations:

▶ Is it possible to leave ownership of the business in the hands of family members in management and leave other assets to your non-active heirs?

▶ If the bulk of your net worth is tied up in the business, does it make sense to give the active family members a majority interest?

▶ Would your heirs prefer to inherit a share of the business or would they prefer to inherit assets outside the business?

▶ Should all offspring own equal shares of the business?

▶ If ownership is to be shared among family members, can they work together without disruptive conflict? If not, what steps can be taken to optimize the quality of their interaction?

▶ Can you work comfortably with those acquiring new ownership positions?

Action Steps:

- ▶ Use your family council to explore family members' desires regarding future ownership of the business.

- ▶ As early as possible, teach the next generation the responsibilities and realities of ownership.

- ▶ Involve outside board members in the process of developing a new ownership structure.

- ▶ Communicate your ownership plan to all members of your family.

- ▶ Actively negotiate evolving roles for yourself and the new owner(s).

- ▶ Ensure that there are exit or cash-out strategies in place for non-active family members.

- ▶ Draft a family shareholder agreement with a buyout clause.

- ▶ Position personal assets outside the business to meet your retirement needs and to provide equitable estate distribution to non-active heirs.

7

Building Your Legacy

To many people, estate planning and succession planning are one in the same thing. We do not believe this to be the case. In our view, succession planning is the overall process that ensures that your best interests, the family's best interests and the business' best interests are all served as you hand off the management and ownership of the family business to your successors.

The more you talk things out, the better the chances that you won't be leaving wreckage in your wake when you finally go to your greater reward!

Like strategic planning, estate planning is a part of that overall process. Like strategic planning, estate planning is an important part, but *only* a part.

A second critical point: to many, estate planning is about minimizing taxes. Period. While death and taxes have been linked forever in that famous old saying, and while reducing taxes is certainly a major part of estate planning, it isn't the *only* part.

And while we're on the subject of death, a third critical point about estate planning: it isn't something you should leave until that time in your life when you start getting "intimations of mortality." In fact, the process should begin when you start your business and continue as both you and the business mature. Over the years, the general goals of estate planning will remain the same:

▶ to create and protect personal wealth,

▶ to ensure that your wealth is distributed according to your wishes, and

▶ to protect the business from the family and the family from the business.

However, your immediate objectives, and the strategies and tools you will use to achieve those objectives, will change over time. The table below summarizes the shift in personal and business priorities as you, your family and the business mature.

PERSONAL STAGE:	EARLY FAMILY AGE 20–35	MIDDLE FAMILY AGE 35–50	MATURE FAMILY AGE 50–65
PERSONAL OBJECTIVES:	Protect family	Build personal wealth	Manage wealth Enjoy wealth
BUSINESS OBJECTIVES:	Survival Stabilization	Create competitive advantage Create business value Build goodwill	Realize goodwill Provide appropriate environment for successor's vision
BUSINESS STAGE:	START-UP	GROWTH	MATURE/ RENEWAL

This chart only covers the "usual" scenario — you start your business and your family when you are relatively young; you grow the business as your children grow up; and you are ready to retire around the time when the next generation is mature enough to take over from you. There are, of course, plenty of other scenarios. You may have started the business in your fifties or waited until late in life to have children. If your situation doesn't fit the "usual" scenario, you'll have to mix and match the items in the table.

Key Question:

One way or another, for a business owner estate planning comes down to a single key question:

▶ How can you leave your family and the business in the best possible financial shape?

Your answer to this question will change over time as the business matures, your family's needs change and your personal financial situation evolves. One thing is sure — you will require the help of a variety of professionals. Your accountant, your lawyer, your insurance agent, your financial planner and your family business advisor can all contribute strategies throughout the process. By the time you are done, you will have been introduced to a wide variety of legal structures, accounting techniques and investment products.

Underlying Issues:

It is beyond the scope of this book to talk in depth about all of the different tools at your disposal in the estate-planning process. What we *can* do is identify five underlying issues you will need to keep in mind when you sit down with your various advisors:

▶ Building net worth outside the business,

▶ Using leverage effectively,

▶ Developing goodwill,

▶ Wise tax planning and investment, and

▶ Linking your plans.

UNDERLYING ISSUE:
Building net worth outside the business

Studies conducted by Arthur Andersen/MassMutual in the U.S. and Deloitte & Touche in Canada indicate that in roughly one in five cases, the business represents more than 75 percent of the value of a family business owner's estate.

This is not a good thing — for several reasons:

▶ Wealth that is tied up in the business is vulnerable — a couple of bad years could wipe out your nest egg and your family's inheritance.

▶ If the bulk of your wealth is tied up in the business, you have no flexibility when it comes to dividing up your estate. You may have no choice but to bequeath company stock to all of your heirs. As discussed in Chapter Six, this could create difficulties in managing the company, and not meet the needs of some family members.

▶ If you leave the bulk of the company's profits in the business, you can create a false economic operating environment by continuing to fund projects and operations that the lending community wouldn't touch.

For these reasons it is a fundamental of effective estate planning that *as the business wealth grows, your personal wealth should grow too*. While reinvestment in the growth of the business is certainly legitimate, once the business begins to show consistent profit, you should try to begin to transfer assets from the business to your personal portfolio.

There are two kinds of assets to target for initial removal:

▶ investment assets — cash, near cash (shares in other businesses), and surplus retained earnings; and

▶ redundant assets — assets not required for operation of the business (boats, cars, planes, vacation properties, and cash).

Frequently, various tax considerations seduce us into purchasing personal-use assets within the business. While this strategy is understandable, it is also wise to create a strategy for removing those assets once they have been amortized and discounted.

Of course the point is not to bleed the business. However, by taking a fair and prudent share of the profit from the business as you go along, you protect your personal wealth from the vicissitudes of business. Furthermore, you allow yourself a more diversified pool of investments, and give yourself greater flexibility when it comes to transferring your accumulated wealth to your heirs.

Explorations:

▶ Have you realized an amount of personal wealth appropriate to your stage in life and the current phase of the business' development?

▶ Have you freed the business from the need to support you in retirement or to support your family after your death?

Action Steps:

▶ Consult with your financial advisor regarding a long-term plan for extracting wealth from the business and strategies for minimizing the tax on the transfer.

▶ Review your business' strategic plan to ensure that it supports your plan for extracting personal wealth from the business.

UNDERLYING ISSUE:

Using leverage effectively

Leverage — borrowing money to make money — is a powerful and versatile tool for expanding your personal wealth and maximizing opportunities for the business. When used effectively, leverage is a good thing. Here's why:

▶ The interest on business loans is tax deductible.

▶ It allows you to extract your retained earnings from the business — as long as you don't have to guarantee the loan.

▶ It allows you to expand the business because the business is in the enviable position of being able to earn you more than the cost of debt service.

▶ It encourages rigorous business decision making.

When you founded your business, you may have borrowed money personally to get started or given your personal guarantee to a business loan. This may be necessary in the start-up stage, but once the business gets on its feet this is an ineffective use of leverage.

Personal guarantees on business loans and lines of credit, and pledges against shares, life insurance and other assets leave your wealth vulnerable and make the business overly dependent upon you. If the business goes under, you stand to lose a major portion of your personal wealth. If you die, the business could find itself in trouble.

As soon as possible, the company should acquire its own loans or line of credit. This frees up retained earnings for transfer into your personal asset pool and allows the company to build a credit, and credibility, rating.

Explorations:

▶ Can you eliminate any non-deductible debt?

▶ Is the business using leverage to take advantage of opportunities for growth or increased profitability?

▶ Are you using leverage to enhance your personal wealth?

Action Step:

▶ Review your personal and business debt with your financial advisor to ensure that you are using leverage effectively.

UNDERLYING ISSUE:

Developing goodwill

Some of the things that have made your business successful are neither fully measurable nor found on the balance sheet. They can, however, translate into dollars when the business is appraised for sale. Taken together, these intangibles are called "goodwill" and it can have an impact on the wealth you ultimately realize from the business.

You create goodwill by paying attention to the existence and development of non-financial assets such as:

▶ a stable employee pool;

▶ appropriately compensated executives;

▶ social capital — positive relationships with your employees, customers, vendors, lenders and politicians;

▶ intellectual capital — like a strategic plan; unique processes or products; knowledge of your products' future life cycles; and your comprehension of your marketplace; and

▶ management competence.

Goodwill is created, grown and matured by different actions at different stages of business maturity.

▶ In the start-up stage, you begin to create goodwill that is largely related to your talents and reputation.

▶ In the growth stage, you work to convert those qualities you have been nurturing into serious competitive advantage — barriers to entry for would-be competitors.

▶ In the mature stage of the business, you work to demonstrate the value of the goodwill the company has developed that is *independent of your personal skills and relationships*. And if you still have some of your money in the business when you retire, you encourage your successors to protect your assets by continuing to maintain and build goodwill.

Explorations:

▶ Have you taken goodwill into account as a long-term asset of the business?

▶ Have you identified and developed ways of measuring the factors that contribute to goodwill?

▶ Do you monitor the company's performance relative to these factors?

Action Steps:

▶ Identify factors that will contribute to goodwill and define ways of measuring the business' non-financial performance.

▶ Set up a system for monitoring the business' non-financial performance.

▶ Seek an appraisal of the value of the goodwill the company has built when you contemplate the sale of the business or the distribution of stock to your heirs.

▶ Highlight the intangibles as you make the transition from the founder to successor generation.

UNDERLYING ISSUE:

Wise tax planning and investment

Minimizing taxes

We have emphasized the importance of turning wealth generated by the business into personal wealth. The problem is that when that wealth is transferred, the government takes a slice. One of your major objectives in the estate planning process is, therefore, to minimize the tax bite.

There are three general ways of minimizing taxes at the point when wealth is transferred from the business to you personally:

▶ income splitting — spreading your income over several family members so that each is taxed at a lower rate than would be the case if a single individual declared the whole amount;

▶ deferring tax — contributing pre-tax dollars to profit sharing or retirement plans; and

▶ changing the nature of the income from a higher to a lower tax bracket.

Governments, unlike individuals or companies, are allowed to double-dip. They will take a further slice of your wealth at the point when it is transferred to your heirs through your estate — unless you take steps now. The general principle is simple — if the wealth isn't part of your estate, it won't be subject to estate taxes (in the U.S.) or probate fees. A good estate plan can maximize the wealth transferred from generation to generation through techniques like:

▶ income splitting,

▶ gifting,

▶ estate freezing,

▶ family trusts,

▶ generation-skipping trusts, and

▶ value discounting through the use of family limited partnerships.

Diversifying investments

The second aspect of wealth management is what you do to grow the wealth you have transferred from the business once the taxman has taken his slice. Your investment planner will have myriad investment products for your consideration and the first piece of advice he or she will give you is to diversify — too many eggs in one basket will leave your portfolio vulnerable.

Mutual and segregated funds, for instance, are now a common method of investing retirement savings. When professionals who sell these funds talk about diversification, they generally mean striking a balance between high-, medium- and low-risk funds. Diversifying your investments should mean much more. The wealth that you take from the business should be segregated into a variety of asset categories so you will have flexibility in what you bequeath to your heirs and to maximize the leverage opportunities of the different types of asset:

▶ investments,

▶ real estate, and

▶ secured operating and shareholder loans protected from personal wealth.

Explorations:

▶ Are you paying the minimum tax on the growth of your personal wealth?

▶ Will your heirs pay the minimum possible taxes on their inheritance?

▶ Are you getting the best possible returns on your investments consistent with your security needs?

▶ Are your personal assets segregated into a variety of asset categories?

Action Steps:

▶ Consult your tax advisor regarding strategies for minimizing the taxes on the wealth you are taking from the business and the wealth that will be transferred to your heirs.

▶ Consult your lawyer regarding the legal structures you can create to support your tax minimization strategies.

▶ Consult with your accountant and/or financial planner regarding a strategy that both grows your personal wealth and provides you with flexibility in how you disperse your wealth to your heirs.

UNDERLYING ISSUE:

Linking your plans

Estate planning is about developing a vision of who will inherit your assets, the form the inheritance will take for each heir, and ensuring that your heirs receive as much of your wealth as possible. However, estate planning for a family business owner does not exist in a vacuum — it is part of a larger process that includes the succession plan for the ownership and management of the business and the business' strategic planning. It is crucial for the sake of the business and for the sake of your heirs that these three plans be fully integrated. This is accomplished through a variety of vehicles, including:

▶ the business' strategic plan,

▶ shareholder and buy-sell agreements,

▶ your testamentary and living wills,

▶ insurance policies,

▶ debt and equity covenants, and

▶ stock option agreements.

It is crucial that they be consistent and support a single integrated strategy.

▶ If, for instance, your shareholder agreement says the business must redeem (buy back) your shares but the strategic plan says that the business will reinvest all retained earnings and cash for the next five years, the business may not have the capacity to meet the terms of the shareholder agreement if you die in the near future.

▶ Or, if the succession plan says your son Albert will control the business but the will says the executors will control the business or select the successor, the business could be rudderless for an extended period while the discrepancy is worked out.

As we said way back at the beginning, all of the many aspects of succession planning are interconnected and require a systems approach. This point bears repeating in our discussion of estate planning, because this is where you focus most on the "hard stop" in the process — your death. Once you are gone, you have no opportunity to fine-tune your planning. If the documents you have created to define what will happen in your absence are contradictory, you risk leaving the business and your family in chaos.

Explorations:

▶ Have you created all of the necessary documents that will define your wishes once you are gone?

▶ Are all of the documents consistent?

▶ Do all participants understand their interdependence?

Action Steps:

▶ Review you strategic plan, shareholder agreements, will, life insurance, debt and equity covenants, and stock option agreements to ensure consistency.

▶ Review all documents with all relevant parties to ensure understanding.

KEY QUESTION:

How will you leave your family and the business in the best possible financial shape?

Leaving your family and the business in the "best possible financial shape" means providing for your dependents without burdening the business. It means using leverage effectively. It means minimizing personal and business taxes throughout your life in business and protecting as much of your wealth as possible at the time of your death. It means developing a diverse personal asset pool so that you have the flexibility in distributing your inheritance to ensure alignment of the management and ownership of the business. It means investing wisely to maximize the wealth you derive from the business.

Money issues

Your answer to this question will evolve over your life in business and will involve a combination of tax and legal strategies, and investment and insurance products and strategies. Outside advisors will play a significant, if not mandatory, role in the development of your estate plan. The table on the following page lists the various types of strategies, documents and products that may be appropriate for your estate-planning needs at each stage of your family's development and the evolution of the business.

Even in this simple table, the sheer volume of considerations can seem daunting — and points to a major pitfall in estate planning. The process requires a variety of specialists, and specialists typically are experts only in their chosen field. The reality is that each is working on a piece of a larger puzzle, and the danger is that each piece can be a masterpiece that unfortunately doesn't fit with the others to make a consistent whole. We therefore can't emphasize enough the value of having a "systems thinker" on board — someone with enough background in each of the many disciplines you will call upon to help keep the big picture in focus and help you coordinate the efforts of all of the specialists.

People issues

Up to this point, we have been talking almost entirely about money. In fact, estate planning is ultimately about people. We haven't focussed on the people end of the process in this chapter because the people issues have been at the forefront in the first six chapters. If you have taken the steps suggested in those chapters, you have a clear idea of what your prospective heirs need and expect from you. You know who wants to carry on the business and who has other dreams. You know who wants an ownership stake in the business and why. You will have worked out who will own and manage the company in a way that balances the family's needs and those of the business. And you will have been communicating constantly along the way with all of

EARLY FAMILY AGE 20–35 BUSINESS START-UP	MIDDLE FAMILY AGE 35–50 BUSINESS GROWTH	MATURE FAMILY AGE 50–65 BUSINESS MATURITY
Current Will–good for 7-10 years	Current Will–good for 7-10 years	Current Will–good for 7-10 years
Shareholder Agreement	Shareholder Agreement	Shareholder Agreement
Buy/Sell Agreement	Buy/Sell Funding	Strategic Plan
		Owner Compensation Plan
		Funded Buy/Sell Agreement
Tax planning	Tax planning	Intergenerational wealth transfer
Income splitting (spouse)	Income splitting-(intergenerational)	Estate Freeze
	Family Holding Company	Gifting
		Trusts
		Entrepreneurial Venture Fund
Savings Plans	Savings Plans	Investments
Life Insurance	Key-person Insurance	Life Insurance to pay estate taxes (where appropriate)
Disability Insurance	Disability Insurance	
Business Loan Insurance	Employee Benefits	Investment Accumulation
	Executive Benefits	

the people who will be touched by your decisions. In short, the people considerations are already covered.

Except for one — communicating your ultimate wishes to your heirs. How many times have you seen this scene in the movies or on television? A breathless family gathers in a lawyer's office to hear a will read...the terms are a big surprise and at least someone in the room is very unhappy. The scene is a cliché, but the fact is that too often it accurately describes the reality. Nowhere is it written that the terms of your will need be a secret until your death. In fact, it is our experience that communicating your plans can defuse many of the family problems that spring from uncertainty.

There is never a guarantee that everyone will be totally satisfied with their lot — but the more you talk things out, the better the chances that you won't be leaving wreckage in your wake when you finally go to your greater reward!

How much is enough?

In a sense, our focus throughout this book has been on avoiding disasters — making sure your business and family aren't left vulnerable or torn apart for lack of adequate planning. Forgive us this deficiency-based thinking — we have seen too many disasters.

There is, of course, another possibility. You may have built up a degree of wealth that more than ensures your family a comfortable future and your successors in the business plenty of room to pursue their corporate visions. If this is the case, you have another question to answer — how much is enough?

Warren Buffet captures your dilemma nicely in his famous assertion that he was leaving the bulk of his fortune to charity because one should leave "enough money to your kids so they can do anything, but not enough so they can do nothing." While Warren Buffet's fortune is extraordinary, the dilemma is not unusual for a large group of people who have created incredible wealth over the last 40–50 years — to say nothing of today's "dot com" millionaires. There are many of you who can give away a great deal of your wealth and still leave behind a vibrant business and a well-off family. You may be concerned about the impact your wealth could have on your offspring's work ethic or upon your grandchildren's values.

Many successful entrepreneurs and family business dynasties are addressing this issue through a focus on philanthropy. A legacy is a lot more than the wealth you leave behind or the business you created. It includes the example you set and the values you instill in the next generation. Creating a foundation or charitable trust as part of your estate plan can enhance your legacy in the broadest sense. On a purely financial level, philanthropy is an effective strategy for minimizing taxes. Beyond that, however, the impact it can have on the community is the kind of personal legacy that often outlasts your business accomplishments. And perhaps most importantly, it can significantly influence your children, and your children's children, and hopefully the world around them.

As with any other course your estate planning might take, communication is crucial — particularly if you plan to give a significant part of your wealth to charity. While being clear about your own desires, keep in mind that the charitable causes your children might prefer to support may differ radically from your own. Whatever the differences, remember that the most powerful way to pass on your values regarding philanthropy is through your own example.

Philanthropy may seem the province of the very rich, but in fact it can enhance the legacy of anyone who thinks twice about what they will leave behind.

Explorations:

▶ Are your dependants provided for in the event of your untimely death?

▶ Would your untimely death create financial problems for the business?

▶ Is your personal wealth keeping pace with the wealth generated by the business?

▶ Have you created diversity in your asset categories?

▶ Have you explored all of the possible ways of minimizing your taxes?

▶ Have you decided who will inherit your wealth?

▶ Have you discussed your heirs' wishes regarding their inheritance?

▶ Have you communicated the terms of your will to your heirs and explained your decisions?

▶ Have you begun the process of intergenerational wealth transfer?

▶ Do your succession plan, estate plan and the business' strategic plan support each other?

▶ What role, if any, do you want philanthropic considerations to play in your estate planning process?

▶ Are there professional advisors or other families in your community to whom you can turn for ideas, suggestions or experience in philanthropy?

▶ Are your children accustomed to organized giving or do they need help getting involved in the charitable community?

Action Steps:

▶ Review your insurance policies to ensure that they are appropriate to the current needs of your family and the business.

▶ Develop a long-term strategy for reducing the business' dependence on your personal wealth.

▶ Develop a long-term strategy for reducing your family's dependence on your personal income.

▶ Develop a long-term wealth management strategy.

▶ Create testamentary and living wills or review your current ones to ensure that they are consistent with your desires, the wishes of your heirs and the other strategic documents of the overall succession plan.

▶ Use your family council to communicate the terms of your testamentary and living wills and discuss your family members' reactions.

▶ Explore with your spouse your personal feelings about the issue of philanthropy.

▶ Consult your attorney or financial planner regarding the use of foundations, charitable trusts or other techniques involving giving in your tax planning.

▶ Explore with your children your intentions and their desires in the area of philanthropy.

A FINAL WORD

There's a good chance you have been feeling a touch of frustration as you have been reading this book. At any number of points along the way, you may have found yourself asking "How?" or wishing there were more detail.

There are tons of books and articles that deal in depth with each of the issues we have raised — you will find a short list of our favorites in the *Resources* section that follows. And in the course of your planning, you will get all the detail and how tos you can handle from the various specialists with whom you will consult.

Our concern has been to help you "see the elephant" when working on any of its parts with any of your advisors.

We certainly aren't implying that your advisors are "blind men," but they will of necessity be focusing on a part of the total puzzle. For you, the challenge will be to stand back and see the overall pattern — and more importantly, to ensure that the parts all fit together. In every one of the situations we have encountered where succession planning has created serious family or business problems, there has been a common pitfall — failure to consider the issues both within the context of the family and within the context of the business.

It is our hope that presenting a wide-angle view of the process will help you avoid this common pitfall.

RESOURCES

General

Cultural Change in Family Firms. Gibb Dyer, Jossey-Bass, 1986.

Effective Succession Planning (2nd ed.). William Rothwell, AMACOM, 2001.

Family Business Review. Volume 3, Number 1, Glenn Ayres, *Rough family justice: Equity in family business succession planning,* 1990.

Generation to Generation. Kelin Gersick, John Davis, Marion McCollom Hampton, Ivan Lansberg, Harvard Business School Press, 1997.

Succeeding Generations. Ivan Lansberg, Harvard Business School Press, 1999.

Systems perspective

Fifth Discipline: The Art & Practice of the Learning Organization. Peter Senge, Currency Doubleday, 1994.

Working with Emotional Intelligence. Daniel Goleman, Bantam Books, 1998.

Working with the Ones You Love – Strategies for a Successful Family Business. Dennis Jaffe, 1991.

Life cycle issues

Corporate Lifecyles. Ichak Adizes, Prentice Hall, 1999.

Managing Corporate Lifecyles. Ichak Adizes, Prentice Hall, 1999.

Seasons of a Man's Life. Daniel Levinson, Ballantine Books, 1978.

Seasons of a Woman's Life. Daniel Levinson, Ballantine Books, 1996.

Management side of the business

Smart Growth: Critical Choices for Family Business Continuity. Ernesto Poza, University Publishers, 1997.

The Dance of Change. Peter Senge, Doubleday, 1999.

Governance in the family business

The Family Business: Its Governance and Sustainability. Fred Neubauer & Alden Lank, Routledge, 1998.

Conflict management and communication

Getting to Yes: Negotiating Agreement Without Giving In. R. Fisher, W. Ury & B. Patton, Penguin, 1991.

Talking from Nine To Five: Women and Men in the Workplace: Language, Sex, and Power. D. Tannen, Avon, 1995.

Workplace Wars and How to End Them: Turning Personal Conflicts into Productive Teamwork. Ken Kaye, AMACOM, 1994.

Web sites of interest

Canadian Association of Family Enterprise (CAFE) (www.cafeuc.on.ca)

Linda K. Fairburn (www.makethingshappen.net)

Family Firm Institute (www.ffi.org)

Mark N. Voeller (www.dialoguesolutions.net)

Young Presidents' Organization (YPO) (www.ypo.org)

ABOUT THE AUTHORS

Mark N. Voeller, Ph.D.

Mark Voeller is President of Dialogue Solutions, Inc., a Dallas-based consulting firm with a primary focus on the complexities faced by families-in-business-together. The son of a second-generation family business owner, and now a non-active third generation owner, he has personally observed and experienced many of the satisfactions and frustrations associated with family business ownership.

Since 1988, Mark has specialized in facilitating leadership succession, organizational communication, and productive conflict resolution within family businesses and professional partnerships. His clients include organizations involved in real estate, distribution, investment banking, ranching, design and retail sales. As an educator, he has taught family systems theory in numerous university settings and published in *Executive Excellence* and in *Family Process*. A member of the Family Firm Institute, he is chairman of its Body of Knowledge Committee.

Linda K. Fairburn, MSOD

Linda Fairburn is an organization development consultant and trainer with a special interest in family businesses. She is President of the Waterloo, Ontario-based consultancy Make Things Happen.

Linda developed hands-on skills in management as the founder and president of companies in the service and manufacturing sectors. Supporting her entrepreneurial capabilities are a bachelor's degree in education and art therapy from the University of Waterloo (BIS), studies in adult education at St. Francis Xavier University, and a Master of Science in Organization Development (MSOD) from Pepperdine University.

Linda brings an entrepreneurial spirit and client's perspective to her work with organizations close to home as well as in the United States and India.

Wayne Thompson

In 1984, a friend offered Wayne "a fast thousand bucks" to write a training video. Of course the job took forever, but in the process he discovered that the skills he had developed in fifteen years of creating television documentaries translated very nicely into designing training programs and corporate communications. He's been doing it ever since as the principal of Summit Run Inc., a Toronto-based training and development consultancy.

NOTES

NOTES

NOTES

NOTES

NOTES

NOTES

NOTES

NOTES

NOTES